NATIVE AMERICAN RITES OF PASSAGE
THE PROCESS OF CHANGE AND TRANSITION

CENTRE FOR PENTECOSTAL THEOLOGY
NATIVE NORTH AMERICAN CONTEXTUAL
MOVEMENT SERIES

Consulting Editor
Corky Alexander

NATIVE AMERICAN
RITES OF PASSAGE

THE PROCESS OF
CHANGE AND TRANSITION

CASEY CHURCH

Cherohala Press
Cleveland, Tennessee

Native American Rites of Passage
The Process of Change and Transition
Centre for Pentecostal Theology Native North American Contextual Movement Series

Published by Cherohala Press
900 Walker ST NE
Cleveland, TN 37311
USA
email: cptpress@pentecostaltheology.org
website: www.cptpress.com

Library of Congress Control Number: 2018952516

ISBN: 978-1-935931-77-5

Edited by Lee Roy Martin

Available at special quantity discounts when purchased in bulk by bookstores, organizations, and special-interest groups.
For more information, please e-mail cptpress@pentecostaltheology.org.

DEDICATION

To My Mother and Father
Mary B. Church-Stevens-Pokagon
(Pokagon Band of Potawatomi) and
Leonard Henry Church
(Nottawasippi Band of Potawatomi)

CONTENTS

Acknowledgements

I would like to show my appreciation to the Brethren in Christ Navajo Mission in Bloomfield, New Mexico and to the Overcomers Alcohol Treatment Program and Staff for their participation in my study. I would also like to say a thank you to the many unnamed clients who offered their input in the questionnaires and in the personal and group interviews. Also, the research could not have been completed without the help from my instructors, Drs Sherwood and Judith Lingenfelter. I appreciate their guidance. They saw the leader inside me and helped to develop that leader. A special thanks goes out to the many Wiconi Family Camp attenders who helped by their responses to the questionnaire. I would further like to say a Migwetch (thanks you) to Raymond and Susan Martel for their editing of this manuscript.

(This QR Code links to the website of Wiconi International.)

LIST OF TABLES

LIST OF FIGURES

LIST OF ABBREVIATIONS

NAIITS	North American Institute of Indigenous Theological Studies
MPI	My People International
IP	Indigenous Pathways
BICO	Brethren in Christ Overcomers
UMC	United Methodist Church
WFC	Wiconi Family Camp
NAC	Native American Church

PART I

INTRODUCTION TO
RITUAL PROCESS AND CHANGE

INTRODUCTION

Background of the Study

As a Native American myself, I know that too often the Christian message and discipleship training have come with the cultural baggage of the non-Native Christians who have worked among Native populations. While spiritual formation is the ultimate goal of presenting Christ's message, the message has often been rejected as the White Man's Gospel. This study examines traditional Native Amerian rituals and demonstrates how these rituals can deepen Native American identity and help Native Christians grow in Christ. The study will proceed within the context of two Native American ministries: The Brethren in Christ Alcohol Overcomers program and Wiconi International and its Family Camp. These contextual ministries have started to help Native Americans see how their own forms can have new meaning in helping them become stronger Christians.

Brethren in Christ Alcohol Overcomers

In the desert Southwest there is a Christ-centered ministry called the Overcomers, which is a residential alcohol treatment program. The program works with Native American men who are in an alcohol recovery program operated by the Brethren in Christ Mission located in Farmington, New Mexico. The program has enjoyed a very high success rate in the number of men remaining alcohol free as a result of the treatment program. It has been estimated that the results of their success range around 70% or better. The program has been in operation since 1997 and has seen approximately 150 men go through the program. The program is unique, as it incorporates the use of Native American prayer rituals and contextualized forms in a Christ-centered Christian program. Another important component of the program is that it is run and staffed by all non-Natives. The Brethren in Christ Mission has been in the area for over 50 years and has been effective in its community relations by working with Native American people who attend the mission's church service and seasonal activities.

I have been involved with this program for the past seven years, and I have helped the treatment program by incorporating my contextualized Christian understanding of the Native sweat lodge and other Native American rituals. The treatment program has found that by incorporating this culturally sensitive approach to ministry, the Native men are more likely to remain alcohol free. The program's unique blending of Native American rituals with a Christian discipleship program connects with the Natives who are in the program. Through God's help, the staff has been able to work with clients in relational aftercare so that the men are able to live an alcohol-free life upon graduation from the program. It is my goal in this project to explore the factors that have led to the overwhelming success of the program with Native American men's continued sobriety and Christian spiritual development.

The rituals and ceremonies that we have incorporated into the program are taken from the Native American traditional world of which I am a part. Through my ministry experience with Native American people and with my work with Wiconi International, I (along with others) have developed several accepted Christianized Native rituals and ceremonies to utilize at the Overcomers alcohol treatment program. What this project will explore is the contextual use of these rituals and ceremonies and their place in the success of the programs ability to help the clients to remain alcohol free upon completion of the program and how the change and transition process affects areas of ministry with Wiconi International. The incorporation of these traditional rites into the Christ-centered program has created a model that can be adapted by other programs that seek to learn more effective methods of treating addictions. What will be further explored is the use of the programs overall model as a rite of passage model of the Native clients' experience with their familiarity with their Native traditional world. The program itself is an example of a ritual in a broad sense, and it will be my aim to show the correlation to ritual and ceremony as it relates to the contextual ministry and the spiritual development of the clients.

Wiconi Family Camp Ministry

Further examination of Native rituals will be undertaken in conjunction with the Wiconi International's organization and Family Camp. The second ministry case, Wiconi Family Camp, is one part of the larger ministry of Wiconi International founded by Native American leader Richard Twiss. Wiconi was founded to empower Native Americans by using traditional forms to instill in them pride in their heritage and to help them grow into stronger Christians. Wiconi teaches that Native Americans do not have to reject their backgrounds in order to follow Christ. After the founder, Richard Twiss, died very suddenly on February 9, 2013, at the age 59, the ministry was plunged into a time of grief and confusion. During that time I was given the role of camp director for the Wiconi Family Camp. I was faced with the responsibility and opportunity to lead Family Camp without Richard's leadership. That year would prove to be quite the challenge for the staff and volunteers, but we were able to make the transition because we had become a team over the years. Despite our grief, we managed to make the Family Camp as enjoyable as possible, giving due respect for the life of Richard Twiss. When at the Wiconi Family Camp, Richard always sat in the same chair while in the auditorium; therefore, to give him due respect, we placed a blanket on the chair to represent his presence. Furthermore, while at the Powwow, we honored Richard by means of the same ritual. Reaching into the traditional culture, we used these created rituals to begin the transition to a Wiconi Family Camp and Powwow without our leader.

Wiconi International was the creation of its founder Richard Twiss who would say that its mission was to bring about a 'preferred Future' to our Native American people. As a result of his motivation to see his vision fulfilled, his preferred future theme would bring about a movement among many Native ministries across the country and the world. To accomplish this, Richard was inspired like many others to reexamine the evangelistic approaches used to minister to the Native people of North America. One of the premises of Richard's approach was to see Native people reached with the gospel of Christ in a manner that retained their cultural identity and that allowed them to follow Jesus fully. For too many years Native people were required by ministry leaders of the day to change and to deny their cultural identity by taking on the culture of the foreign missionaries. To oppose this mind set, Wiconi set out to begin a conversation among the Native church world to accept a new approach called Culturally Appropriate Ministry to indigenous peoples. This approach is also referred to as Contextualization. In contextualization, the indigenous peoples' cultural ways are viewed as appropriate expressions of worship that may be utilized in ways that honor our Lord Jesus Christ. As a result of this conversation, Wiconi became a hub around which many Native ministries sought partnership both formally and informally. Consequently, Richard became very well known nationally and internationally for his ideas and methods. Out of his approach to ministry was born the Wiconi Family Camp. The Family Camp is now into its twelfth annual event and is held at the Aldersgate Methodist Camp in Turner, Oregon, in late July each year. The camp begins on Thursday afternoon and ends at noon on Sunday and is attended by Native and non-Native people from the region and across the United States and Canada. My family and I were not part of the first camp but became regular ministry presenters from that time forward. Richard was intrigued with the method I used in the construction of the sweat lodge, and he appreciated the way I conducted the ceremony inside the lodge. Further, while Richard was attending an event in Albuquerque, New Mexico, my church conducted a Powwow in the sanctuary of my home church, and he then wanted us to help with his Powwow at the next Family Camp. Over the years, Lora and I have become respected leaders in Albuquerque and have experienced several opportunities to be head dancer in Albuquerque and in other communities across the country.

The Wiconi Family Camp, as it relates to this research, has to do with the approach and methods used to promote contextual awareness and the practical application of the many rituals and ceremonies practiced among many of the tribes of North

America. This is the central focus of this project. As a result, at the Wiconi Family Camp we have created over the years many acceptable Christianized Native American traditional rituals and ceremonies. Our camp attendees are able to experience these rituals as examples of contextualization, and they learn to apply Wiconi's approaches into their ministry context. The adaption of these various rituals and ceremonies and their relations to the spiritual development of the camp attendee is what I referred to as rites of passage, which will further add to the focus of this project. Rites of passage are found among many indigenous peoples around the world and even within the European peoples, of which some examples will be explored. Some of the rituals and ceremonies Wiconi has developed as contextual authentic Christian expressions include: the sweat lodge, the use of incense in prayer, dancing at the Powwow, singing with the traditional Powwow drum, and the smudging ritual. Other rituals will be referred to within this project as examples of how Native people are able to adapt other personal and familial rituals and ceremonies from their cultural ways associated with life experiences as they relate to Christian spiritual development. These will include such rituals and ceremonies as: a baby's first laugh, puberty rites, becoming a dancer, and leadership status changes.

The BIC Overcomers and the Wiconi Family Camp provide opportunities for research on the importance of ritual and liminality for contextualizing the Gospel in order to help Native Americans grow in Christ. This research will further provide an in-depth look at the use of ritual and ceremony as it relates to the concept of rites of passage as developed by Victor Turner in *Ritual Process*, in which he explores the functional use of rituals among indigenous peoples as methods of managing life situations.[1] In addition, I have learned much from this research that will guide me as I have accepted the invitation to lead Wiconi International as its director for the next phase of its ministry.

---

[1] Turner, *The Ritual Process: Structure and Anti-Structure* (1966 Lewis Henry Morgan Lectures; New York: Aldine Transaction, 2011).

Historical Context of Native American Ministry

This history of evangelism among the Native North Americans since the early days of contact, dating back to the 1600's, has been an example of the intrinsic forces within the human psyche. The need to reinforce the dominant people's view of biblical history has shown itself around the globe as indigenous people were subjugated by those more powerful. It is called ethnocentrism, which is the belief in the superiority of one's own cultural group.[2] If we know what ethnocentrism is and how it affects the way we succumb to its influence on us individually and with our social systems, we can begin to sort out cultural knowledge from biblical understandings. In the religious realm, it also raises its ugly head even in the cultural bias that surrounds things like church planting. In part, it is ethnocentrism that causes non-Natives, when establishing churches in Native America, to transfer their culture to these new churches.

Missionaries around the world plant churches in other cultures and attempt to make them identical to the churches in their home countries. Sherwood Lingenfelter calls this condition 'culture bound', causing many obstacles to mission work. He writes,

> Yet all Christian leaders, regardless of their cultural background, carry their personal history and cultural biases with them wherever they serve. Most current traditions of leadership are culturally bound and when applied in a cross-cultural context, those traditions become obstacles to effective ministry.[3]

He also notes, 'Missionaries have succeeded in bringing a biblically informed worldview but one that is thoroughly contaminated by their culture'.[4] Therefore, is it possible to bring a truly transformed gospel if we are always limited to reducing our own cultural reflection of Christianity wherever we carry the message?

---

[2] *American Heritage College Dictionary* (Boston, MA: Houghton Mifflin, 1985), s.v. 'ethnocentrism'.

[3] Sherwood G. Lingenfelter, *Leading Cross-Culturally: Covenant Relationships for Effective Christian Leadership* (Grand Rapids, MI: Baker Academic, 2008), p. 15.

[4] Sherwood G. Lingenfelter, *Transforming Culture: A Challenge for Christian Mission* (Grand Rapids, MI: Baker Academic, 1998), p. 12.

When working among Native Americans, I start with a new focus. Paul G. Hiebert and R. Daniel Shaw advise: 'This new focus is not a project to be accomplished through human engineering and action. It begins with learning to understand people deeply, identifying with them, and building relationships of love and trust.'[5] Richard Twiss agrees:

> This is a time of transition in ministry among indigenous be-lievers around the world – a time of exploration and sincere inquiring of the Lord for new perspectives and approaches to Native ministries. Around the globe among indigenous Chris-tians, cultural identity is surfacing as the key dynamic in this emerging new Native ministry paradigm and spiritual awaken-ing.[6]

This time of transition has opened many doors for many minis-tries across North America and Canada and around the world to have hope for the indigenous church's desire to reach our own people, using forms they identify with. However, the movement toward contextualization has not come without opposition. Many Native ministries, whether operated by Native or non-Native staff, are trapped in the paradigm of the rightness of European ethno-centric practices over their religious lives.

One of the aims of this study is to reveal the the advantages of process, change, and transitions as a natural and needed ap-proach to facing many of the desired changes shown wanting among Native American organizations and ministries. Despite this desire, though, the dark cloud of conformity continues to hang over us. Sherwood Lingenfelter states: 'The social and cultural sys-tems a missionary creates among local indigenous communities exert powerful pressure on new believers and churches to con-form to habitual standards, values and practices'.[7] This pressure has carried over as we are aware of the many pressures our mod-ern churches face every week. 'Rather than worship or evangelism,

---

[5] Paul G. Hiebert and R. Daniel Shaw, *Understanding Folk Religion: A Christian Response to Popular Beliefs and Practices* (Grand Rapids, MI: Baker Publishing Group, 2000), p. 11,

[6] Richard Twiss, *One Church, Many Tribes: Following Jesus the Way God Made You* (Ventura, CA: Regal Books, 2000), p. 19.

[7] Lingenfelter, *Transforming Culture*, p. 18.

a church can fall prey to thinking that its purpose is keeping up a tradition, holding a particular event, or maintaining a building. These are good activities but they do not make up our purpose.[8] Jesus Christ gave the following commission to his disciples:

> Therefore, go and make disciples of all nations baptizing them in the name of the Father and of the Son and of the Holy Spirit, and teaching them to obey everything I have commanded you. And surely I am with you always, to the very end of the age (Mt. 28.19, NIV).

This scripture one day opened my eyes to my failure.

Once I devoted my life to serving God, I focused on the cultural awareness and the freedom we had to utilize our own indigenous culture for God's glory. Over the years, have found many others also had this focus as well. As a result of this project, my research, and subsequent findings, it became very apparent to me that while I was inclined at first to become more Christ-centered in our approach, what I was really seeking in this phrase was to become more focused on discipleship and spiritual development. As leaders in Native American ministries, we must help the contextual ministry movement participants to center on their new identity in Christ and lead them through the process of commitment to Christ and to one another, enabling them to be the people of God on mission together. The focus of this project is to see all of life situations, the ministry at the Brethren in Christ Overcomers, the Wiconi International organization, and the personal leadership development as a process of change and transition. To accomplish this, I will use Victor Turner's concept of rites of passage and liminality, in which people move from structure to anti-structure and to structure again. The middle period, anti-structure, he labels liminality, a time when labels are stripped away and people can build a sense of community with each other not founded on structural distinctions like power or gender.

---

[8] James Emery White and L. Ford, *Rethinking the Church: A Challenge to Creative Redesign in an Age of Transition* (Grand Rapids, MI: Baker Books, 2003), p. 31.

Transition, Change, and Liminality

We all realize that the world is not the same as it was in biblical times. Change and transition are a natural process of life and history. I have studied the numerous changes that have occurred throughout Christian history, and I acknowledge that every culture where the gospel entered underwent challenges to adapt the message contextually, thus contextualization is as old as the gospel itself. Contextualization is the vehicle that made the rapid spread of the gospel possible, until it stalled when reformers settled on what they thought were the ultimate modes of Christian expression. Today, indigenous peoples around the world are awakening to their freedom to adapt the gospel to their cultural context. Where they can, as the scripture states from Mt. 28.19-20, they 'go and make disciples of all nations baptizing them in the name of the Father, Son and the Holy Spirit' and teaching everything that Christ commanded. Indigenous discipleship utilizes methods that better meet the individual's cultural needs. This is what we as indigenous people see as our ultimate challenge from Jesus Christ. The goal is not to use our cultural way as the end in itself. The goal is not to focus primarily on contextualization. Rather we must use contextualization as the vehicle to allow us entry into people's world through their hearts and minds in order to present Jesus Christ in a manner more natural to indigenous people. The contextual movement is not intended to be a passing trend but a serious approach that will overcome the ineffective approaches of the past. In the past I have focused too much effort on contextual approach development. Now, I seek to take those created cultural forms and focus on their use for making disciples and for increasing spiritual development.

Through the use of contextual approaches, I have grown in my personal spiritual life, and I have also grown to trust God fully with my life. The journey to trust God fully has been a challenging area for me. Yet the journey has been periodically interrupted by criticism from conservatives who regard contextualization as a form of syncretism. Many Native Christian leaders firmly resist and oppose the efforts to create a world where Native Americans can expression their Christian faith in a manner more closely allied to their worldview. The integration of the Bible from a Non-Native perspective has no connection to culture as if all of Hebrew tradition were fully western. Their view of authentic Christian expression from the Native World must look, act, sound, and feel like today's western church models. These western church methods have experienced dismal results in Native evangelism, with less than 5 % of Native Americans identifying as Christian. This is after 450 years of western-style evangelism.

Because of these past dismal results, the Brethren in Christ Alcohol treatment program has chosen to conduct their program from a fully contextual approach. Now the program is experiencing approximately a 70% success rate among Native men who seek alcohol treatment. The program continues to change lives, with many of the men accepting Christ as their personal savior. With all of the opposition and resistance to change, my question is, where are their successful treatment programs? The results of the Brethren in Christ program speak for themselves. Results do not happen without change and transition, but with any changes, the process has come with a beginning, a middle, and an end. This process extends into all areas of life, even with those who oppose the type of contextual changes. I have known several individuals who were very much opposed to contextual methods, but who, after investigating the issues more fully, have ended up as supporters of contextualization.

The BICO program itself has built within it the change process. The men come to the program, which is an ending of one part of life as they knew it, and the beginning of a new phase of life. The three months in treatment is a middle time, where new ways of living are taught. This is the liminal period, a time where change can take place. The process then terminates with an ending of the program, but the beginning of a new way of life, called reintegration. This process is a natural Native traditional way and is a common experience many Native people are familiar with in their personal family lives. This change process can be seen in puberty rites, community status change, and in becoming a man or a warrior. William Bridges writes, 'while the changes we are facing differ from any we've experience before, the transition process by which people get through change is well mapped'.[9] Native people have developed rituals and ceremonies to cope with these changes and transitions.

What is change and how do we bring it about? Making the transition through changes is a major part of this study. The clients at the Overcomers alcohol treatment program are moving from being trapped in the swamp of drugs and alcohol to an in between time of relearning life from a Christian worldview, to stepping into the same world with a whole new life focus. This experience is exactly what happens in a rite of passage. In the same manner, ministries and organization can move through such stages and emerge on the other side of change ready to face the world. The desired outcome is to create changes that will impart the future.

Rick Richardson, in his book entitled, *Evangelism Outside the Box*, says, 'Every ministry born in the 1960's or before probably needs significant and sometimes painful soul-searching change, especially in the area of its sacred practices in order to thrive and be fruitful today'.[10] These words are full of distain for ineffective forms that for too long have controlled the only approaches to ministry around the world. The issue at hand is this, are we doing all we can to disciple and advance the spiritual development of the lost? Dean Gilliland in his work entitled, *Paul's Theology and Mission Practice*, makes note of the need for change by saying,

> The important point that underlies this is that Paul's churches were meeting the special needs of natural groupings of people and were communicating the gospel in relevant forms and in languages that were suitable to each group and place. Those churches of Paul's ministry were not foreign or strange. They were flexible, open fellowships deferring in style and form, yet committed to basic teaching and features of worship that identified them all as one.[11]

---

[9] William Bridges, *Managing Transitions: Making the Most of Change* (Boston, MA: Da Capo Press, 2009), p. x.

[10] Rick Richardson, *Evangelism Outside the Box: New Ways to Help People Experience the Good News* (Downers Grove, IL: InterVarsity Press, 2009), p. 23.

[11] Dean S. Gilliland, *Pauline Theology and Mission Practice* (Eugene, OR: Wipf and Stock Publishers, 1996), p. 210.

To ensure that this type of ministry would take hold and become a movement, Paul learned the process of transition and change and used it fully.

For clients at the Brethren in Christ, for organizations like Wiconi International, and for leadership development in times of transition to happen, change and transition must take place. Similarly, for change to take place almost anywhere – especially in our Christian church world – we must begin to realize that ineffective methods must be modified and revised so that they can be effective once again. Neill and Chadwick observe, 'The old non-Christian past must sink below the horizon. That which has come from the west must be so absorbed and assimilated that it can be transformed and re-expressed in categories different from those of the world of it origin.'[12] To accomplish this has not been an easy road, but many mission-minded thinkers have suggested ways to make it happen. One of these was Paul Hiebert, who responded to this challenge with his concept of critical contextualization. Looking at the Native American traditional world through Hiebert's kind of critical eyes has reinvented the work with the Brethren in Christ alcohol treatment program. The same can take place in Wiconi International and in the road of leadership I have been given. Unfortunately, however, we often occupy ourselves with doing business and management as usual, so that we take little time or effort to think ahead of the curve. Looking ahead must include the realization that transition and change are a part of life and that within the Native American worldview all of life is sacred; that is, it is full of ritual and ceremony. In the contextual ministry realm, life becomes an experimental process with ceremony, and these ceremonies are developed to bring about a desired end. In a world of transition and change

> framing everything as an experiment offers you more running room to try new strategies, to ask questions, to discover what's essential, what expendable, and what innovations can work. In

---

[12] Stephen Neill and Owen Chadwick, *A History of Christian Missions* (New York: Penguin Books, 1990), p. 398.

addition, an experimental frame creates permission and therefore some protection when you fail.[13]

Statement of the Research

The initial purpose of this study is to examine the factors involved in the success of the Brethren in Christ Overcomers alcohol treatment program as these factors relate to the recovery and spiritual formation of the clients. More specifically, I will focus on the use of contextual Native American prayer practices as one definite avenue toward the clients' spiritual development and subsequent sobriety.

Research Problem
The problem of this research is to investigate how the use of Native American rituals in two contextual ministries, alcohol treatment and Family Camp programs, creates a liminal spiritual experience for the participants that leads to freedom in Christ and to deeper spiritual formation for the participants.

Sub-problems
1. To discover and analyze how the staffs at the BIC and Wiconi International perceive the effect of using Native cultural forms incorporated into their Christ-centered alcohol treatment and Family Camp programs.
2. To discover and analyze how the participants perceive the approach used by the Brethren in Christ Overcomers program and the Wiconi Family Camp program as it leads toward their freedom from past addictions and toward camper spiritual formation in Christ.
3. To compare how Native prayer practices and rituals were used as a natural component of these programs' overall approach to the ministry for addiction recovery and to the camping program in developing spiritual formation.

---

[13] Ronald A. Heifetz, Marty Linsky, and Alexander Grashow, *The Practice of Adaptive Leadership: Tools and Tactics for Changing Your Organization and the World* (Cambridge, MA: Harvard Business Review Press, 2013), p. 277.

4. To compare how the staff and participants at each program responded to the use of biblical teaching and Christian beliefs in these ministries.

Methodology

Through participant observation, individual interviews, and questionnaires, I will gather data on the methods used in the Brethren in Christ alcohol treatment program and the Wiconi Wacipi Family Camp. I will develop case studies to elicit personal responses from the Family Camp's and treatment program's staff, clients, and campers in relation to these programs' unique approach to alcohol treatment and Christian Family Camp. I will use the three data collection methods to triangulate the data.

CHAPTER 1

FOUNDATIONS FOR THE RESEARCH

The overarching theme of this project has to do with how change and transition are handled by individuals and groups, especially within the Native American world and/or within organizations and ministries working with Native American people. The study of the Brethren in Christ Overcomers treatment program revealed how Native men enter the program with life-controlling addictions, but after proceeding through the three-month program, they subsequently exit the program with a positive outlook to life without drugs and alcohol. As a result, seven of ten men continue a life free from the prison of addiction. The process that clients encounter in BCO parallels many of the Native American rituals and ceremonies that they had encountered in their Native traditional world. These similarities point to valuable connections that suggest a useful paradigm in which to analyze the data, methods, and approaches of the Native men's alcohol treatment program. This paradigm also relates to most any type of change and transition that individuals and organizations face.

Victor Turner and the Ritual Process

Through his book, *The Ritual Process*, I gained an appreciation for Victor Turner's work that examines liminality and community as well as their relationship to the individual and society. While working through Turner's own thoughts, I gained insight on the relational side of change and transition. Turner was not satisfied with the approaches that other researchers used to the study cultures. He was especially dissatisfied with the way rituals were analyzed. He concluded that an outsider could not adequately engage in research of another culture and could not fully represent the beliefs and rituals of another culture. Seeing the way other researchers were conducting research, Turner chose to utilize the indigenous informant, stressing the inner meaning of the ritual being studied. He was conscious of the way researchers were implanting their own thoughts into the indigenous person's explanation. Finally, it was his final chapter titled, 'Humility and Hierarchy', that Turner's work relates directly to my situation, as I enter a new leadership position that engages the change and transition that the Wiconi International organization has entered.[1] Earlier, Victor Turner wrote a work dealing with the process of change and transition entitled, *The Forest of Symbols*, in which he looks deeply into change and transition and the processes involved.[2] Although the concept of 'rites of passage' is credited to Arnold van Gennep,[3] Turner focuses on the transition period of initiation rites of the transitional time, which is called the liminal phase. In his essay, 'Betwixt and Between: The liminal Period in *Rites de Passage*', Turner offers insights and concepts that connect more with rites of passage issues.[4] Here is where Turner makes a useful connection to my study.

Arnold van Gennep defined 'rites of passage' as rites which accompany every change of place, state, social position, age, and most all areas involving change and transition. Van Gennep notes that this process is marked by three phases: separation, marginal or limen, and aggregation. Turner prefers to 'regard the transition as a process, a becoming, and in the case of *rites de passage*, even a

---

[1] Turner, *The Ritual Process: Structure and Anti-Structure*.
[2] Victor Turner, *The Forest of Symbols* (New York: Cornell University Press, 1967).
[3] Arnold van Gennep, *The Rites of Passage* (London: Routledge, first published 1960, reprint edn, 2004).
[4] Victor Turner, 'Betwixt and Between: The Liminal Period in *Rites de Passage*', in June Helm (ed.), *New Approaches to the Study of Religion: Proceedings of the 1964 Annual Spring Meeting of the American Ethnological Society* (Seattle, WA: University of Washington Press, 1964), pp. 4-20.

transformation'.[5] Turner restates van Gennep's three stages as Separation, Liminality, and Reintegration. These stages can be seen at the Brethren in Christ Overcomers alcohol treatment program and in the organizational changes Wiconi International is encountering. They also relate to the life situation of leadership transition in an organization I am encountering. The schema of van Gennep and others have shown that rites of passage are not confined to culturally defined life-crises but may accompany any change from one state to another. These could include such areas as relocation, conversion, loss of loved ones, and recovery after a natural disaster. My study has shown that rites of passage also include transition out of addiction, organizational change, and passing of the leadership baton.

These various times of transition and change can be placed into what Turner calls rituals and ceremonies. Rituals are closer in association with social state, which is where rituals are transformative and ceremonies are more confirmatory. Turner states,

> Even as imitation in tribal cultures must relinquish former structural ties. Undergoing nakedness, poverty, and complete submission to the terms of liminal passage in order to attain the next life stage, so the individual in our own culture must leave old ways behind, divesting oneself of ego's claims to rank and social function, in order to attain a more highly individuated stage of growth.[6]

Liminal Studies in Christian Ministries
Allen Roxburgh states,

> Rites of passage are rituals, usually religious in nature, through which individuals are detached from their established and normal role in society by being placed outside the social nexus in an in-between state; and after some ritualized passage time,

---

[5] Cited by Louise C. Mahdi, Steven Foster, and Meredith Little, *Betwixt & Between: Patterns of Masculine and Feminine Initiation* (Peru, IL: Open Court, 1987), p. 287.

[6] Victor Turner, *The Forest of Symbols* (New York: Cornell University Press, 1967), pp. 3-6.

they are returned, inwardly transformed and outwardly changed, to a new place and status.[7]

Roxburgh shows how the Bible's narrative is full of rites of passage stories involving beginnings, ends, and in-between stages. He notes,

> Liminality is in every chapter of the scriptures and so is ceremony. Ceremony marks the beginnings of an end, and liminality experiences in scripture often had these processes and results. In both Hosea and Exodus, the desert is the place where Israel entered the most profound reshaping experiences of God. It was in these liminal areas that the potential for a new future was forged.[8]

Roxburgh further says,

> Victor Turner describes three phases of transition in the rite of passage process. Separation, liminal, aggregation. Examples of this are seen in the lives of the Hebrew people when they: Enter Egypt / Time spent there / Exodus. Then again as they leave Egypt, they once again go through the processes as they: Leave Egypt / Time in the desert / Enter the promise land.[9]

The Hebrews of scripture were tribal people, and many of the situations in their lives are similar to those of the Native Americans. 'As Native people, we are in-between the worlds of yesterday and where we will be, between traditional worldviews and the western rationalism, between community and individual, between spiritual and religious.'[10] These places are neither good nor bad, it is only part of life, and they require time to learn from them for they are primal states, familiar to all cultures in which new beginnings can emerge.

---

[7] Alan J. Roxburgh, *The Missionary Congregation, Leadership, and Liminality* (New York: Bloomsbury Academic, 1997), p. 24.

[8] Roxburgh, *The Missionary Congregation, Leadership, and Liminality*, pp. 27-31.

[9] Roxburgh, *The Missionary Congregation, Leadership, and Liminality*, pp. 27-31.

[10] Richard Twiss, 'Rescuing Theology from the Cowboys: An Emerging Indigenous Expression of the Jesus Way in North America' (DMin diss., Asbury Theological Seminary, Wilmore, KY, 2011), p. 35.

In *Transforming Culture*, Sherwood Lingenfelter argues that culture and worldview are not natural, but they control the way we react to our social world. He writes that 'transformation means a new hermeneutic – a redefinition, a reintegration of the lives of God's people (the church) within the system in which they find themselves living and working'.[11] He relates this control to those who are unknowingly trapped within our own cultural prisons. For transformation to take place new methods, approaches, and ideas must be attempted. William Bridges concurs: 'When you're in transition, you find yourself coming back in new ways to old activities'.[12] These times are indispensable if change is to occur. The stages of separation, liminal, and reintegration begin. Bridges describes the liminal time as the neutral zone. The neutral zone is not just meaningless waiting and confusion. It is a 'time when reorientation and redefinition is taking place'.[13] Liminality is necessary, and in western understanding and Native American understanding the liminal 'is a moment out of time and out of secular social structure, a limbo of status-less-ness. A liminal state is often seen as sacred, powerful, holy and a set apart time in which the old structure, rules of order, and identities are suspended.'[14] The research at the Brethren in Christ Overcomers alcohol treatment program shows that the liminal state has been incorporated into the methods of the treatment program. Regarding the clients in the BICO program,

> contextual methods brought new understanding into their lives as Native followers of Jesus that resulted in longing for liberty, wholeness, and a sense of creator's affirmation as tribal and indigenous people. These new ideas were not passing fads of novelty. They stuck and created change.[15]

The Brethren in Christ Overcomers alcohol treatment program utilizes Native American traditional prayer practices as a

---

[11] Lingenfelter, *Transforming Culture*, p. 19.

[12] William Bridges, *Managing Transitions: Making Sense of Life's Changes* (Boston, MA: Da Capo Press, 2004), p. 7.

[13] Bridges, *Managing Transitions: Making the Most of Change*, p. 90.

[14] Paul G. Hiebert and R. Daniel Shaw, *Understanding Folk Religion* (Grand Rapids, MI: Baker Academic, 2000), p. 297.

[15] Twiss, 'Rescuing Theology from the Cowboys', p. 134.

natural part of the treatment's approach. Most importantly, however, these indigenous expressions of Christian faith must be firmly rooted in the teachings of Scripture and the living Christ. The local culture must be examined phenomologically to understand its beliefs – the ideologies upon which people act.[16]

Ritual Process and Change

Contextual methods are now being used widely throughout North America and in many areas around the globe. Changing times and new mind sets have opened the door for allowing new approaches, such as the rites of passage rituals, to be used. Through their use, indigenous people are finding wholeness and balance that has been missing. People face crucial periods in their lives, which cause transition and change to be a common occurrence. 'As individuals grow up within the family and reach critical stages of transition, members hold rites of passage for those individuals to initiate them into the new stage of structured relationship.'[17] In utilizing these traditions, organizations, individuals, and churches are beginning to find their God-given place in the body of Christ, thereby putting life into a harmony with the world. The many Native nations across North American have such ceremonies – the Navajo of the southwest call this Hozhoo, 'being in harmony'. Change presents the choices either to resist it or to embrace it, and either way, we encounter consequences. 'Life does not afford unlimited time and opportunity, so we must seriously consider the high cost of change versus no change.'[18] Scripture reveals cases when change came slowly, even when the people of God were under the leadership of divinely-appointed representatives like Moses. At one point, Caleb, Joshua, and others could not convince the majority to move, and so they wandered in the wilderness for 40 years, and a generation had to die before they took the land that God had promised.

Many individuals, organizations, and ministries are not looking to change; and there is no effort to seek out new methods or

---

[16] Hiebert and Shaw, *Understanding Folk Religion*, p. 21.

[17] Lingenfelter, *Transforming Culture*, p. 167.

[18] Alan Nelson and Gene Appel, *How to Change Your Church (Without Killing It)* (Nashville, TN: Word Publishing, 2000), p. 136.

approaches to create new and better ministries, structure, or leadership. Instead, the mission is often simply to maintain the status
quo. Like keeping an old car that should be put to rest, we do
minor fixes to keep the car running. In many cases, we do only the
minimum, washing the windshield, checking the fluids, adjusting
tire pressure, and waxing the outside. Stagnant types of organization would prefer to stay in an old method with little result rather
than to make the needed changes. God would honor and give favor to new and more effective methods, but change is risky and
requires trust in God. Therefore, when an organization gets to a
point where they know they are not doing all they could to advance the Gospel of Christ, they need to step into a period of
change and accept a rite of passage phase in their ministry.

In his seminal work on leadership, Bill Hybels observes from
his own experience that there are starting points, mid-points, and
ending points in ministry.[19] William Bridges describes these stages
in different terms, noting that every ending starts a new beginning,
middle, and ending; and this cycle continues over and over.
Bridges further notes, '[T]ransition is different. The starting point
of dealing with transition is not the outcome, but the ending that
you'll have to make to leave the old situation behind.'[20] In order to
accomplish this I heard it said, 'You can't get to where you're going
until you leave where you've been'. Transition to a new way of
doing anything is always hampered by the attitude called the seven
last words of a dying church: 'We never did it that way before'.
Ministries and organizations that on the edge of failure must take
seriously the issues and dynamics related to change and transition.

As it relates to the Brethren in Christ Overcomers treatment
program and the use of traditional prayer practices in a Christian
ministry, we had to consider the extent to which these practices
could be be adapted in the Native Christian context. Paul Hiebert
argues that the response of new converts to their adopted Christian faith always relates to their cultural past. Christianity will in-
tersect with any number of a convert's pre-Christian cultural elements, which were taken for granted before the gospel was heard.

---

[19] Bill Hybels, *Courageous Leadership: Field-Tested Strategy for the 360° Leader*
(Grand Rapids, MI: Zondervan, 2012), p. 43.
[20] Bridges, *Managing Transitions: Making the Most of Change*, p. 8.

We must ask how far the gospel can be adapted to fit into the culture without losing its essential message. Moreover, we must ask, 'Who should make these decisions?'[21] I have found these concerns to be very relevant to the situations of change and transition that I have encountered over the past two decades (and even more so as I enter a position of leadership). Dancing on the edge of authority is a scary place, whether that authority is a formal authority derived from Scripture or an informal authority given by an organization. The challenge is further complicated, because the boundary is not fixed in stone. The only way we know that we are dancing on the edge of our scope of authority is by the degree of resistance we encounter when we make a move.[22] Resistance can come from several directions. There are those who want to maintain the power, those who oppose any new approach to ministry, and those who are overly impulsive to move in any direction other than the familiar. In the contextual ministry approach, I agree with the following: 'Where clear biblical principles contradict cultural values, the Bible takes precedence, but where the Bible leaves room for flexibility, the cultural values of the local host culture should normally prevail.'[23]

---

[21] Hiebert and Shaw, *Understanding Folk Religion*, p. 183.
[22] Heifetz, Linsky, and Grashow, *The Practice of Adaptive Leadership*, p. 283.
[23] James E. Plueddemann, *Leading Across Cultures: Effective Ministry and Mission in the Global Church* (Downers Grove, IL: InterVarsity Press, 2009), p. 89.

Chapter 2

Ritual Process and Change – My Personal Story

I am a Pokagon Band Potawatomi member of southwest Michigan. My Potawatomi name is Ankwawango, which means 'Hole in the Cloud'. I am of the Bear clan from my mother's side, the late Mary Church (Pokagon), a Pokagon Band Potawatomi member and the Crane clan from my father's side, the late Leonard Church, Nottawasippi Huron Band, both from Michigan. My wife Lora (a Navajo) and I are in the midst of raising five children in Albuquerque, New Mexico where we have lived since 2000. My journey in contextual ministry created a desire for me to study under traditional elders where I learned many of the traditional spiritual teachings of my Anishinaabe people of the Great Lakes region. I also studied at Grand Valley State University, where I examined the culture and religion of Native American peoples and where I earned a Bachelor of Science degree in anthropology. I received the Master of Arts in Intercultural Studies degree from Fuller Theological Seminary in Pasadena, California where I studied culturally appropriate (contextualization) approaches to Christian theologizing in the Native American context. Finally, I earned the degree Doctor of Inter-cultural Studies, also at Fuller Theological Seminary, and this monograph is a slightly modified version of my doctoral dissertation.

From 1996 to 2000, Lora and I served in Grand Rapids, Michigan, as pastors of a Native church plant that would become one of the first Native American contextualized worship services in the country. Lora and I have also led Native Christian ministries in the southwest, where we continue to minister today. I have been a presenter at national and regional conferences dealing with Native ministry topics. Currently, I minister with the Brethren in Christ Overcomers alcohol treatment program where I conduct a Christ-centered contextual sweat lodge ceremony and provide guidance in contextual ministry methods to the staff at the mission. I have served as a consultant and interim staff for the General Board of Global Ministries of the United Methodist Church's office of Native American and Indigenous Ministries. Further, I am a board member with NAIITS, the North American Institute for Indigenous Theological Studies and a contributing writer for its academic journal and a workshop presenter at its symposiums. I am a devoted father and husband to Lora, a Navajo from Albuquerque. Finally, I have ministered for 16 years with Wiconi International of Vancouver, Washington, an organization founded by the late Richard Twiss (Rosebud Lakota/Sioux), and I have accepted a position as Director of Wiconi International where I will work with Wiconi staff and colleagues to help take the organization into the future.

Prior to accepting the Wiconi director position, I made my living as a carpenter, working with various businesses such as Goodwill Industries. I also worked for a general contractor for 10 years in Albuquerque. All of my life has prepared me for the work in which I am currently involved. But before this life-change in ministry, I was a weekend warrior (as I like to call it), where I held a full-time carpentry position and was involved in ministry on the weekends. Having resigned my secular employment as a carpenter, I now work for the Master carpenter, Jesus Christ.

In 1992 I had an experience so powerful that it divided my life into the 'before' and 'after'. I was a college student taking classes in English, and while completing an assignment, I wrote about my struggle to understand the separation of spiritual worlds in my life. What I was experiencing was the beginning of what I learned later was called contextual ministry. As it turned out, I was ambushed, and through the combination of the class assignment and the Holy Spirit, it was revealed to me that there is a way to be fully

Native and fully Christian. This all happened in a serendipitous dream/vision experience. In this dream/vision I had awakened from sleep and had dreamt and seen while awake an event that could only have come from God. I sensed the Holy Spirit telling me not to leave this thought/experience but to listen to God, to think about what I had just seen, to consider the implications, and to let my heart be grabbed by the reality of the moment.

The dream/vision led to a journey in contextual ministry that had its start in a church plant in Grand Rapids, Michigan, in the mid 1990's. This church plant began with two Anglo men who ran an after-school mentoring program for elementary and middle school students. One of these men was a former missionary to Muslims and a teacher at Cornerstone University, and the other was a music major at a Cornerstone University as well. Their program was growing, and there were even some adults starting to attend. They were feeling God leading them to transform their program into a Christian ministry outreach. In the course of events they eventually asked me to pastor this ministry, which turned into a successful church plant. The church plant was unique in that I was being led by God during this time to begin incorporating Native traditional rituals and ceremonies as authentic expressions of Christian worship and prayer. What resulted was the creation of one of the first contextual ministries in the country. The ministry met in a rented facility on Tuesday evenings and had an average of 50 in attendance.

With my motivation to use cultural practices, we began to attract the attention of the local churches in the area – some were supportive; some were not so supportive; and others were totally against our initiative. With the help of several ministry friends and relatives, we sat and discussed what was taking place in our ministry. What resulted was the affirmation that what we were doing was right in the eyes of God and needed to be done. When we opened the doors for our first service, we had already made some significant changes in the traditional approach to church planting. The Native cultural expressions that we incorporated into worship included the use of the Native drum as a musical instrument, and the arrangement of seating in a circle. Further, I dressed in a Native styled ribbon shirt, and I preached while sitting down. We would open the church service with the burning of incense that Natives call smudging, which is the fanning of the smoldering smoke of sage. Beyond these practices I would conduct other church related services such as funerals and wedding – and even the Eucharist – with the use of the sacred Native Pipe Ceremony. Our service as mentioned ran 50 in attendance. We did not know it at the time, but we were on the high end of attendance for most Native ministries in the country. Through this church plant I learned that God was pleased with our ministry approach and with the methods we were using as expressions of our Christian faith. I further felt God leading me to go beyond these and also incorporate the Native sweat lodge. Moreover, even our participation in the Powwow dancing became a natural part of our Native Christian world. In the Native world, the sweat lodge is a place of prayer where rocks are heated in a fire and placed in a dome shaped lodge structure, and water is poured on the hot rocks to create a steam so that there is a cleansing of the participants both spiritually and physically. Dancing at the Powwows was just a natural part of being a Native person in our Native community. Dance at our gathering was an acceptable social and spiritual practice and was enjoyed by many. Through it all we felt a closer relationship with our creator Jesus Christ. We later discovered that there were a few other ministries like ours across the country.

My spiritual growth during this time took me to places I never dreamed I would go. After we had been conducting services for about a year, I received a phone call from a cousin who told me with excitement to turn on the television to the Trinity Broadcasting Network. I did as she asked, and on the screen was a man being interviewed who was wearing a full Plains Indian regalia with headdress. I watched with curiosity as he shared the same message that I had been teaching about the need to create a new approach to Native ministry. This was the first time I heard of Richard Twiss. Up to this time, we thought we were the only ones attempting this type of ministry experiment. Now, with this television program, my curiosity was peaked, and I took down the contact information and made plans to call him the following week. I called the Wiconi International's office, which was located in Vancouver Washington. I said as he answered, 'this is Casey

Church of Grand Rapids, Michigan, and I caught your interview the other night' and … At this point in our conversation Richard said, 'Let me say something.' The first thing Richard Twiss said to me was, 'we have heard all about you and your work in Grand Rapids, and I want you to know, you are not alone'. We further shared for a time in a friendly conversation. This was my first meeting with another person outside our group who was speaking the same language.

With this first conversation we started a relationship that could only have been made in heaven. I became more involved with his ministry and was asked to join him and some others in an event called Many Nations One Voice conferences, known as the MN1V. With these events my ministry world was opened up to several of the main leaders in this new contextual movement. I met such leaders as Terry Leblanc and Randy Woodley. From the meeting of these and many other likeminded ministers, we soon became a close ministry family. As time went on Richard planned to do a camp in Oregon where he and others would create an environment where families could come and experience a Christianity expressed from within the Native American culture and worldview. My family and I did not attend this first event because we were involved in the tremendous undertaking of relocating to Albuquerque, New Mexico, in 2000, where Lora's family lived. After getting settled into our new home and community, we again became more involved in the ministry of Wiconi.

We were asked to come to Wiconi International's Family Camp in 2004 and to be a part of the support staff. We were invited to join the staff, in part, because of our knowledge of culture and traditions. Furthermore, our family was a fine example of a contextual family, and Wiconi was looking for partners they could trust. Now, many Native American ministries were getting more and more involved in contextual style ministries. Many of them sprang up fast and wanted to join in as soon as they could. They wanted to get on the bandwagon and ride on the popularity of Richard Twiss and all the attention the Wiconi organization was getting. Many wanted to join for the wrong reasons and some were very eager but were not fully ready theologically. During this time, Lora and I sat with Richard and his wife Katherine at the Wiconi

Family Camp in the gazebo. We said to them that we were feeling drawn by the Holy Spirit, and we would like to partner with them more fully than we had been to this point. Richard and Katherine were honored to have us join them, and as I look back, I can see that Richard was preparing us for a bigger role than just Family Camp. He planned to create an organization that would be a lighthouse to many Native American ministries and communities. To do this he was also nurturing others, like us, along the way.

My leadership style and strength grew as I was asked to be a board member with NAIITS, the North American Institute for Indigenous Theological Studies. At this time, Richard was the chairmen of NAIITS, and he asked me to join them as a board member. I also became more involved in the planning and implementation of contextual forms at the Wiconi Family Camp. At the camp, I was given the responsibility to build and teach the construction of the sweat lodge because of the unique way we were constructing it and because of the way we were conducting the ceremony in Albuquerque. I further accepted the task of seeking out those who would conduct the sweat lodge ceremonies while at the Family Camp. I also worked with the setup and coordination of the Powwow which took place on Saturday afternoon and evening. Each of these responsibilities helped me to grow in knowledge of the Wiconi Family Camp and in the ability to take on tasks within my comfort zone. These efforts made me more visible among the staff and volunteers at the camp, and I soon was able to manage many other jobs at the camp.

In the midst of everyday activity in ministry, I also grew in my understanding of who we were and how I could best serve within the Wiconi organization. The years of serving God in Wiconi under Richard Twiss' leadership were some of the most precious times of my life. Our efforts have not gone unnoticed, and whether I knew it or not, some began to notice something in my character and life that I did not know was even there. Although I sought to do the best possible job in every task asked to do, I always submitted to the leadership of Richard and the Wiconi staff. Contextual ministry was in my makeup, and I seem to grow more and more in my capabilities at Family Camp, with the Brethren in Christ Mission, and everywhere I focused my ministry attention. After completing my Masters in Intercultural Studies at Fuller Theological Seminary, I still had the desire to continue my studies. In 2007 I applied to Fuller Theological Seminary's School of World Mission for the PhD in Intercultural Studies and was accepted. I had in mind to focus my studies in this program on the rituals used by the Hebrew and the Native American people and look at the comparison between the two as they related to the use of incense and rituals. I also became interested in how the Hebrew people adapted various forms from the surrounding pagan culture's influences and see how this might influence my work with Native American people. I chose this topic because I am a Native insider in this process and may have a unique view to this topic. I have been deeply involved in re-traditionalizing the rituals used by my Native people, having adapted the sweat lodge and the use of the Pipe in my Christian expression of faith. Doctor Daniel Shaw was to be my mentor and was very excited to work with me. In a conversation, I explained to him my journey and what I hoped to accomplish while in the program. During our first class time at the Fuller campus, we began to narrow down our research topics, and we all had to present our anticipated focus to the group. I mentioned how I wanted to look at the use of incense rituals, and I had working title for my study. I wanted to title it 'Holy Smoke'. At that, the group applauded and wanted to know more.

After only a couple of classes, the tide of economic change was taking place across the country, and it did not look bright. I had been working as a carpenter for a local contractor for over a decade, providing for my growing family and as a tent maker or, as I like to call it, a weekend warrior for God. As a carpenter, I worked full-time, but every weekend I would seek out various ways to make an impact for Christ among Native Americans in our region. I enjoyed the weekend warrior way of ministry and also my employment as a carpenter. In the spring of 2008, the economy fell, and this effected my employment when my employer had to lay off twenty-four of my fellow workers, including me. As a result, I made the choice to withdraw from the Fuller PhD program at great disappointment to my mentor Doctor Shaw.

Economic times across the country got worse, and any type of employment was hard to find. We became a typical story of a family meeting the challenges of making it through this very hard time. Lora and I managed to keep the house and to keep food on the table and clothes on the backs of our five children. Times eventually got better, and the house and jobs were now secure. Through it all, I remained as active as possible in ministry at the Brethren in Christ mission and with Wiconi Family Camp. Lora and I were not able during this time to help with the cost of coming to the camp, having put all of our resources to sustaining our home and family life. Because of Richard's desire to have us maintain a presence at the camp and to stay involved, Wiconi financially made it possible for us to attend for several years. With the economy shifting to better times, we maintained our relationship with Richard and with the Wiconi Family Camp. It was during this time I felt I could return to my studies at Fuller and still maintain our family and home. I made some calls and spoke to Doctor Shaw and eventually returned to Fuller. I returned not to the PhD, but I chose instead the Doctor of Missiology. I was accepted into the program and began my studies in a cohort with Doctors Judith and Sherwood Lingenfelter. I began my studies with the cohort with a similar direction – to study rituals in Hebrew and Native American cultures. This direction changed with a focus on the Brethren in Christ Alcohol treatment program and the changes happening with the men as they were able to go through the program and continue to remain alcohol free as a result. This became my research topic and the new focus of my studies.

More Changes Ahead

With the sudden passing of Richard Twiss in the spring of 2013, I volunteered to work with the Wiconi Family Camp, having been involved with the camp for the past ten years. I felt I could add my leadership to making the camp continue for this first year without Richard. The Wiconi board agreed, and I took up leadership as the Wiconi Family Camp director. Leading up to the second Wiconi Family Camp, I was asked to think about stepping up even more in leadership and took on some of the speaking engagements that Richard would normally do. After the second Family Camp, I was asked by the Wiconi board to come on board as staff. This meant not only being the Family Camp director but also filling in on several other commitments Wiconi had for this year, which included teaching with Sioux Falls Seminary's Immersion Class held in South Dakota on the Rose Bud Sioux reservation in mid-July.

Transition and change have become a part of my ministry life, and now another major change was unfolding. In January of 2015, I was asked to come to Vancouver, Washington, to meet with the Wiconi board, who were to offer me the position as the Director of Wiconi International. Now Lora and I had brought our family life and household to a very stable place and were very confident that life was going to be much better. However, I was met with a decision to step into a position of an uncertain future with Wiconi, an organization that was going through great change and transition. I accepted the offer, and the world of Casey Church was yet to take on more change and transition.

PART II

CASE STUDIES OF RITUAL PROCESS AND CHANGE

CHAPTER 3

THE BICO ALCOHOL TREATMENT PROGRAM

Data Collection Methods

In preparation for my research, I made plans to interview the staff and clients of the alcohol treatment program. Upon receiving permission to conduct my study, I made arrangements to participate in a program to observe their approach and to interview the staff and clients at the program individually and in groups. I prepared a preliminary questionnaire to elicit information ('fishing') from the staff and from the clients.

To conduct my observation of the sweat lodge and of the contextual church service, I was an active participant in both. In observing the treatment programs approach in the center, I relied on the staff's responses to the preliminary questionnaire and interviews. The data collected from the field notes suggested to me certain areas on which I should focus the final form of my questionnaire, which I then constructed and administered.

Conclusion: The questionnaire subsequently revealed that the factors leading to the client's success in recovery were due only to the contextual methods used in the program's approach to alcohol treatment.

Table 1: First Attempt at Data Collection, 'Fishing'

Code	1	2	3	4	5	6	7	8	9	10	11	12	13	14	15	16	Total Hits	% of group
Contextual Items	7	10	12	11	10	2	1	1	1	3	3		2		3	1	14	87 %
Social Areas						1	1	2	1		1					1	6	37 %
Prayer Rituals	1	1	1		2	3	4	2	3	5	7	2	10	5	5	1	13	81 %
Spiritual Formation	2	5	7	5	4	2	2	2	1	2	4		2		2	1	13	81 %
Native Identity	9	1	8	6	3	1	1	3	1	2	2		6	1	4	1	12	75 %
BIC Program		2	7	6	6	2	1	3		3	3			1	3	1	12	75 %
Neg. view ofWestern	6	2	5	5	3	1	1	3			1		1	1	5	1	11	68 %
Sweat Lodge	1	1		5	1	1	1		2	1	5		2		1	1	11	68 %
Contextual Music	1	2			1	2	2	1	3		1	2	2		2	1	13 %	81 %

The chart above (Table 1) represents my first attempt at data collection, which was obtained through the questionnaire. This attempt was eschewed in favor of a second, more narrow analysis that searched only for contextual items used at the treatment program. I was biased in my first analysis and leaned heavily toward looking for factors relating to contextual items. I was unaware of my bias and was made aware of it by my professors. As a result, I sought to re-analyze the data with a total rereading of the data collected and with a more objective view toward the responses collected. This first attempt was a learning experience in conducting research. Being a novice in research, I grew in my understanding of data collection and analysis and this data is presented here to illustrate an inappropriate approach to research. The data I will use for this study will come from my second attempt at analyzing the data collected.

The data in Table 2 below reflect a more balanced and objective approach to data analysis, not the biased approach that I had utilized in the first attempt.

In collecting the data for this second attempt for a more objective approach, I did not change my questionnaire or the responses I received from the staff and the clients. The data I collected in the first analysis was still adequate for this re-analysis. The only difference is in the way I went about analyzing the data this time. I had been made aware that in my first analysis I had looked at the data with a biased eye, and I had found only what I wanted to find in the data.

The second analysis of the data from the responses of the questionnaire revealed very different findings. I observed from the data many of the same contextual items, but beyond these, the data also showed many other items. The chart above indicates findings of one or more responses of the coded items from each participants. If an item was not mentioned, I did not indicate it on the chart, but if it was mentioned, then I gave it a mark of one. Some respondents noted the items many times, but I still marked it as one, noting that they observed it as an important item in the program's approach rather than giving it a mark for each time they

Table 2: Re-reading and Re-analysis of Same Data

Code	1	2	3	4	5	6	7	8	9	10	11	12	13	14	15	16	Total	% of Group
Importance of family	1	1	1		1	1	1	1	1	1	1	1		1		1	11	68%
Faith Development	1	1				1	1			1	1	1		1		1	11	68%
Life Skills Training	1	1	1		1	1	1	1	1	1	1	1					11	68%
Sense of Healing		1			1	1	1	1	1	1	1		1	1		1	9	56%
Christian Bible Study		1				1	1	1	1	1	1		1	1		1	9	56%
Christian Belief Values			1	1	1	1	1	1	1	1	1			1	1	1	7	43%
Christian Relationship			1	1			1	1		1	1	1		1	1	1	10	62%
Native Christian Identity	1	1	1		1	1	1		1	1	1			1	1	1	10	62%
Importance of Classes				1		1	1	1	1	1	1	1	1	1	1	1	10	62%
Program Style	1	1	1		1			1		1		1		1			8	50%

noted it. There were other factors noted by the respondents, but I only noted those factors that been mentioned by at least 43% of the respondents. This data analysis revealed that the program had many other factors beyond the contextual items that I had noted in the first analysis.

Conclusion: As a result of re-analyzing the data with a more balanced and objective approach, I concluded that the factors contributing to the Brethren in Christ alcohol treatment program's successful recovery rate (and the rate at which clients remained drug and alcohol free) were related to the program's Christian approach and the Christian relationships found at the program. This finding was further confirmed by the group interviews with the clients. My first analysis had concluded falsely that the primary success factor was the program's incorporation of contextual approaches, but that was not the main recovery factor. However, the second analysis shows that the contextual approaches were secondarily important and that they added to the clients' overall positive views of their Native identity. As a result of incorporating contextual methods to their religious lives, the clients obtained a more positive view of being able to live a Native and Christian life together. Moreover, some clients found growth in their spiritual formation through the contextual rituals. To reiterate, the contextual rituals and ceremonies were found to be valuable, but they were not the main factor in the clients' successful recovery. When asked in the group interviews what they thought were the most important aspects of the program that led to their being able to remain alcohol free, they responded by naming the ten items listed in the chart above.

The data collected in Table 3 below show another very important set of responses beyond those found in Table 2 regarding the factors leading to the success of the client's recovery. This table is the result of seeing even deeper into the data. After our doctoral cohort's third class module on Change Dynamics, I was struck with the image of rites of passage, which deals with change and transition dynamics that take place in what is called the liminal phase. With the same data as before, I once again re-analyzed the responses of the participants to the same questionnaires. After

Table 3: Data for Rites of Passage Theme

Theme	1	2	3	4	5	6	7	8	9	10	11	12	13	14	15	16	Total	% of Group
Enter and Exit	1	1	1	1	1	1			1		1	1	1	1	1	1	13	81%
Isolation for 3 mo.	1	1	1		1		1				1		1			1	8	50%
Feeling healing	1	1	1	1	1		1	1	1		1	1	1	1		1	13	81%
New Information	1	1	1	1	1	1	1	1	1	1	1	1	1	1	1	1	16	100%
Seeing New Identity	1	1	1		1		1	1	1		1		1		1	1	11	68%
Ritual and Ceremony		1	1	1	1		1	1	1	1	1	1		1	1	1	13	81%
Change and Transition	1	1	1	1	1		1	1	1	1	1		1	1	1		13	81%
In Between time	1	1	1	1	1		1	1	1		1		1	1			11	68%
Feeling of being changed	1	1		1	1		1	1		1	1		1	1	1	1	12	75%
Rites of Passage	1	1	1	1		1	1	1	1		1	1	1	1	1	1	14	87%

further research into the processes involved in rites of passage, I
became more attuned to the process. With this deeper understanding, I went through the responses once again, this time in
search of the theme dealing with rites of passage and those images related to separation, liminality, and reintegration. The chart
above reveals what I found in the data dealing with the rites of
passage. Each mark on the chart shows when the participant
noted some aspect of the rite of passage images and those related
processes involved in change and transition that take place in liminality.

With this new analysis of the data, I discovered that the rites
of passage process was also a factor that enabled successful completion of the alcohol recovery program. The rites of passage process can be seen in many areas of our lives: in our mental, physical,
emotional, and spiritual lives. With this theme revealed, I was able
to apply it to the change and transitions taking place at the Brethren in Christ Overcomers alcohol treatment program, the Wiconi
organization, and in my personal leadership development.

Conclusion: The data suggests that the clients' success in their
recovery from alcohol addiction is due in part to the rite of passage aspect of the treatment program. The Brethren in Christ alcohol treatment program is a ceremony, a ritual in which the clients enter, go through a liminal phase, and then reintegration takes
place with their graduation from the program. The three areas of
rites of passage are evident in the programs structure and also in
the Wiconi Family Camp structure. This topic will be further explored and expanded in a subsequent section.

Brethren in Christ Overcomers

The research at the Brethren in Christ treatment program had its
inception with my involvement in its design and in its approaches.
The program began in 1997 and was very similar to most any
other treatment program in the country. At the beginning, the program showed little success. When Duane Bristow became the new
director, he was willing to take the program in a new direction, but
he was not sure how best to make improvements or what needed
to change. In 2001, Duane Bristow and I met at the leadership
conference held by the Nazarene Indian Bible College in

Albuquerque, New Mexico. From that point, we worked together to create the program that we have today. The program now has a very successful recovery rate of men leaving the addiction of alcohol, a success rate not seen in most programs. However, the improvements did not come easily; they required courage and the willingness to take risks to create a better future.

Since 1997, the program has operated in much the same manner, although we have added several program approaches we thought would make the program even better. Features of the program that have remained constant include the use of the same main program and staff, the use of home living coordinators, and my participation as the cultural advisor who provides the Native ritual to the program. The program utilizes the same Bible study material, although some of the teachers have changed. The program has been at the same location, and only cosmetic changes have been made to the facilities. The program maintains a low number of clients for each session, ranging from 6 to 8 per session. The home living coordinators vary but are mostly made up of volunteers from the Brethren in Christ churches from the Pennsylvania region. Since 1997, the program has served approximately 150 Native men. Over the years, some of the clients have become part-time volunteers in the program. There is now an active search for a facility near Farmington, New Mexico, that would serve as a half-way house. The staff believe that, if built into the program, such a facility would further improve the recovery rate.

A certain amount of risk was involved in making the changes to the program that I have mentioned, and these types of risk run against the grain of many denominational traditions. History has shown that an ethnocentric model has been used to evangelize many Native peoples around the world, a model that denies the local cultural expression as an acceptable expression of indigenous Christian faith. The approaches of the western church have sought to reshape the 'receiving' culture into a replica of the 'sending' culture, and this model is still continuing to this day. In response to this approach, I have heard Richard Twiss say many times, 'Why should Native people give up their sin-stained culture only to replace it with another people's sin-stained culture?'

With this said, the many risks taken at the Brethren in Christ Mission and the Overcomers alcohol treatment program are just these, cultural risks. When I first became involved with the Overcomers, the director and I met to discuss the need to make contextual changes in our approaches to Native ministry. As a result, I was invited to work with the Brethren in Christ Mission, a relationship that opened the door to experimentation in ministry methods. To begin, we allowed the topic of contextualization into our conversation, a freedom that was not allowed before. From that point, we sat and opened the door to what could not or should not be allowed as acceptable adaptions of Native culture. As they relate to the current approach, we worked to incorporate into the worship methods items common to the Native cultures, such as sitting in a circle while at the Sunday church service, the postured adopted in most Native meetings. We also allowed the minster to sit instead of standing at the pulpit. Furthermore, we adopted the burning of incense in certain rituals, such as in the blessing and in the prayer ceremonies used by the Native people. However, the use of incense in church services is not new, inasmuch as the Roman Catholic and Orthodox churches have used it throughout history. One last item incorporated into the Sunday church service is the use of the drum as our primary musical instrument. Singing with the drum, we utilize a playlist of new songs created for this new way of ministering. This new genre of music incorporates several Native tunes sung with Christian lyrics. The songs are easy to learn, especially for the Native men, because the tunes are familiar to them. Over the years I have learned that there are no Christian songs – there are only Christian lyrics.

As it relates to the Overcomers program, we went further by incorporating the use of the sweat lodge. The sweat lodge is a cultural place for prayer, cleansing, and teachings. The lodge is not a spooky pagan ritual that should never be used in the Christian world. It is a very acceptable ceremony. It is similar to a sauna that could be found at any health club, except that it is made of mostly natural material and heated with rocks from an open fire. Similar to the fitness club sauna, the lodge is used for physical cleansing but goes further to incorporate the mental, spiritual, and emotional aspects of life. Many Native cultures use the sweat lodge, and each has it traditional way to conduct the ritual. Our sweat lodge ritual is conducted by believers in Christ and not by a person who does not profess faith in Christ. Our addition of the sweat lodge to the alcohol treatment program is an example of success- ful transition and change. We entered this phase of liminality ready to take risks, using sacred items in a manner acceptable to Native culture but also acceptable to our Christian faith.

Risk taking has always presented itself to me, I have never sought it out. To accomplish our task at the Overcomers program we had to take some risks. But first we had to motivate and en- courage the denominational leadership and the program staff to trust God and to trust us as we experimented with a variety of new approaches. Our laboratory would be the treatment center and the ministry of the Brethren in Christ mission. In this labor- atory, we were willing to try anything with the guidance of the Holy Spirit. Many of the new approaches were made up on the run; and in these cases we relied on the view of Heifetz, who says, 'Leadership is about improvisation',[1] making it up as you go. The liminal phase that we entered was our time to take risk, the kind of risk that we hoped would change lives. 'When you really don't know what to do, all you can do is become an artist. The motive for creative leadership is not a matter of whimsy, it a matter of survival, making the future work.'[2] Being an artist myself has helped me to be creative and willing to innovate and improvise. This ability to create was also exercised in the planting of a unique style of church, designed for Native American people in Grand Rapids, Michigan, called, 'All Tribe Gathering'. To travel in un- charted waters is scary, but we truly believe that we had God's favor. 'Ministry from the fringe, where few resources and no prec- edent exist, means that visionaries are both freed and forced to innovate.'[3] When we entered this time, we knew we were entering a liminal phase with many challenges before us. Our approaches were not popular or accepted by most Christian religious leaders at the time, but we moved forward without their permission. 'But you may need to push beyond the boundary at least a bit by

---

[1] Heifetz, Linsky, and Grashow, *The Practice of Adaptive Leadership*, p. 104.
[2] Heifetz, Linsky, and Grashow, *The Practice of Adaptive Leadership*, p. 207.
[3] Plueddemann, *Leading Across Cultures*, p. 58.

challenging norms that inhabit-progress. You might need to take action and then ask for forgiveness rather than permission to run the experiment.[4] The following table illustrates some of the changes we encountered as we created the approach used at the Brethren in Christ Mission and the Overcomers treatment program.

Table 4: The Ritual Process of Contextual Prayer for BICO

Sacred Rituals	Liminal Experience	Meaning for Participants
Sweat Lodge: done in a contextual way	The incense burning blessing the clients and the lodge. Heart-felt prayers are said. The feeling of the cleansing spiritually and physically take place.	The sense of the sacred is created between the clients and God. The hearts of the clients find a connect better in the lodge than when sitting in a room.
Singing with the drum with contextual lyrics	It is a learning time for the clients. The drum becomes a central part of the recovery process. The drum become a way to sing their worship to God. They hear the Christian lyrics in the songs. The drum becomes a natural way to sing theology	The drum becomes instrumental in the recovery process because of the relationship the clients have made with the staff and home living coordinators.
Praying with incense done in a contextual way	This a learning experience for the clients. They hear positive words from a Christian leader concerning the use of incense. When the incense is lit, blessing and prayers are done. A feeling of normalcy is entered by praying in their Native way.	The clients learn they can pray in a Native way to Jesus. The drum becomes a central part of the program. A Native self-identity begins to foster spiritual growth.

The Brethren in Christ is a unique place for my study because it uses methods found in other Christ-centered recovery

---

[4] Heifetz, Linsky, and Grashow, *The Practice of Adaptive Leadership*, p. 283.

programs, but it also incorporates Native American cultural practices into the program. In order to accomplish their high recovery success rate while using Native American practices, they had to make the adaptive challenge journey through many changes and transitions. 'Adaptive challenges require new learning, innovation, and new patterns of behavior.'[5] The Brethren in Christ demanded more than changes in regular routine or practices. They wanted and sought for change of mind and heart that would challenge and transform long-standing habits and deeply held beliefs. These strong beliefs may be referred to as cultural prisons. Dr Lingenfelter notes that we need to comprehend the dimensions of our cultural prisons, and discovery comes from the biblical keys that will allow us to unlock the chains of our own cultural habits and the gates to our own cultural walls.[6] My journey in ministry has profited greatly from the understanding of these cultural prisons, as I worked with a group in Michigan and created many unique expressions of Christian faith from within the existing Native American culture and within Wiconi International. When working with the Brethren in Christ, I was able to help them create expressions fitting to the Navajo culture and traditions. Dr Gilliland, in 'Paul's Theology of Mission', notes similar approaches to mission work, 'The greatest gift a missionary or mission agency can give to a young church is the right to think out and act out the Christian life for itself'.[7] Working toward an expression fitting of a truly indigenous church image is our goal. The staff and I see our work as being a mediating work of Christ within their own environment. This mind set has created an attitude and a habit within the ministry to embrace new approaches. However, for solid change to continue to take place and for the improvements and ideas to be secure, they must become a part of the culture of the ministry. Exercising this courageous approach leads to a point of no return, when old ways of the cultural prison no longer overpower the new ways that are being developed.

---

[5] Sharon D. Parks, *Leadership Can Be Taught: A Bold Approach for a Complex World* (Cambridge, MA: Harvard Business Review Press, 2013), p. 10.

[6] Lingenfelter, *Transforming Culture*, pp. 19-20.

[7] Gilliland, *Pauline Theology and Mission Practice*, p. 221.

The Brethren in Christ program has made this move and has become a ministry that is courageous enough to embrace needed changes, and these changes have overflowed to all areas of their ministry. The transition process too, has developed new and creative approaches, but these have come as a result of having an experimental mind set. We have learned that a great deal of the so-called spiritual development has nothing to do with older approaches used in treatment of alcohol addiction. Rather, growth comes through facing behavioral problems biblically and relationally, with ritual and ceremony.

Change and transition bring about an understanding of old approaches as they have been applied to the Christian religion. By examining the former rituals and ceremonies created by our European ancestors, we can understand how culture-bound they had become. Having taken their cultural expressions of the Christian faith to the world in their own form and style, it is no surprise then that Christianity was often seen as foreign religion, and Christian converts became aliens in their own land. This is the world where I minister in the southwest, and it holds true in many other areas of the country as well. Many non-contextual churches maintain the forms taught to them by years of ministry from this foreign approach. Charles Kraft notes that more often than not, the majority of reservation churches essentially 'maintain the foreign forms, imposing them on new generations', and they end up with little regard for the fact that the forms they impose have very different meaning to new generations.[8] However, hopeful changes have taken place, and we are transitioning to a new approach to Native ministry, moving from the culturally restrictive to the culturally inclusive. Richard Twiss states that 'a result of prolonged colonization is that our people have fallen into a state of liminality where living in transition has become our enduring reality'.[9]

---

[8] Kraft, Charles H., *Appropriate Christianity* (Pasadena, CA: William Carey Library, 2005), pp. 32, 70, 459.
[9] Twiss, 'Rescuing Theology from the Cowboys', p. 35.

CHAPTER 4

CASE STUDY: WICONI WACIPI FAMILY CAMP

Research Methodology for the Study of the Wiconi Family Camp

The chart below (Table 5) illustrates the responses from Wiconi Family Camp attenders. The research at the Wiconi Family Camp consisted of interviewing ten camp attenders regarding their perception of the Family Camp. The study proceeded much like the previous exploration of the factors leading to the success of the Overcomers Alcohol Treatment Program. This study explores the factors that the attenders of the Wiconi Family Camp believe makes the Family Camp a continued success for the past ten years. With this study, the same sub-problems will be used in order to keep the focus of the study controlled.

Selection of the ten camp attenders for this study began with a questionnaire that was given to twenty camp attenders. Of the twenty questionnaires sent to camp attenders, fourteen responded. To narrow the number to ten participants, I chose the ten that had answered all the questions completely. I then analyzed the responses of these ten campers, attempting to avoid the problem of bias fishing that had distorted my first analysis of the Overcomers program.

The results of this analysis show success factors that are similar in some respects to the success factors in the Brethren in Christ Overcomers study. The data from the questionnaire reveal that the

Table 5: Success Factors at Wiconi Family Camp

Code	1	2	3	4	5	6	7	8	9	10	11	12	13	14	15	16	Total	% of Group
VIP of family & Relations	1	1	1	1	1		1	1	1	1	1	1		1	1	1	14	78%
Powwow & Social Time	1	1	1			1	1	1	1	1		1		1	1	1	10	62%
Pos. effect of faith Development	1	1	1	1	1	1		1	1	1	1	1	1	1	1	1	14	78%
Sweat VIP for Healing	1	1	1	1		1	1	1	1	1	1	1	1	1	1	1	12	75%
Biblical Info. Very useful	1	1	1	1	1	1	1	1	1	1	1	1	1	1	1	1	12	75%
Singing with Drum vip	1	1	1	1	1	1	1	1	1	1	1	1	1	1	1	1	16	62%
Native & Christian Identity beneficial	1	1	1	1	1			1	1		1	1		1	1	1	12	75%
Strong sense of family vip	1	1	1	1	1	1	1	1	1	1	1	1	1	1	1	1	16	100%
Ritual &Ceremony sacred time	1	1	1	1	1		1	1	1	1		1	1	1	1	1	13	81%
Program Style	1	1	1	1	1			1		1	1	1		1	1	1	8	50%

participants gave very sensitive and friendly responses to my questions. The questions I used for this study required only a minor reworking of the language found in the questions that I had used in the Brethren in Christ Overcomers study. In most cases, I only had to change the name of the program to make the question suitable for this second study.

The following is a short description of the responses given by the attenders of the Wiconi Family Camp held at the Aldersgate Camp and Retreat Center located in Turner, Oregon. One prominent response indicated an appreciation for the camp's emphasis on the importance of family and for the Christian relationships that were made while at the camp. We strive to make the camp as family-friendly as possible. The camp is advertised as a Family Camp and those attending are made up of many of the families who are directly involved in some form of Christian ministry. In the beginning, the camp was a place for these ministers to meet and get to know other minsters who were also struggling in the trenches with contextual ministry. Due to the makeup of the camp attenders, many of them are ministered to and grow deeper in relationship to Christ and to each other. Along with the relational feel to the camp, another important aspect of the camp was the social life we created in the Powwow. The Powwow was open to the public, and those who attended felt the same family-friendly atmosphere that was evident in the entire camp. The Powwow features many dances that are geared toward getting the audience involved. The inter-tribal dance is a time for everyone to participate, and those participating can dance with or without regalia. Other dance offered is the switch dance, where a woman dancer will place her shawl on the back of a male friend or a guest and that person has to dance the women's style. This creates a fun and enjoyable time with much laughter. One other dance is the potato dance, where a couple will place a potato between their foreheads and try to dance without the potato falling. The winners are the last couple still dancing with the potato between their foreheads.

The spiritual benefit of the camp is enhanced by the presentation time, in which invited speakers share their experience in ministry. These presentations are filled with biblical examples from Scripture, and they give the attenders a real boost to their faith journey. In 2014, the camp's theme focused on the music ministries of several of our contextual minsters. I asked the speakers to speak to the good, the bad, and the ugly aspects of their ministry journey and end with a positive reflection on their ministry experience, sharing the many beneficial features of contextual music ministry journey. These presentations give the attenders a look into the real-life situations of the musicians, and in so doing help build the attenders individual faith journey.

The cultural teachings presented at the camp include the use of the sweat lodge, which includes the history and the construction of the lodge. The camp attenders are encouraged to participate in one of the sweat lodge ceremonies conducted by some of the minsters. In particular, I offer a sweat lodge ceremony for beginners. In this ritual for beginners, I keep the heat in the lodge lower than it would be for those with more experience in a ritual sweat lodge. Along with the beginners sweat, I offer a healing sweat, which I offer as a co-ed sweat, where both male and female and both young and old can attend. In this ceremony, my wife and I help the attenders open up to some of the mental, physical, emotional, and spiritual issues; and we pray for them in the sweat lodge. As a result of this ceremony, the attenders feel a sense of healing that helps them in their spiritual development.

One aspect of our program is the use of Native musical instruments. These include the flute and drum. The drum has been a fixture with the Wiconi Family Camp from the beginning. In the western Christian world, the drum has been given many negative connotations that made Christians fearful of using it in worship. At the camp, the drum is prayed over, and the songs sung on it have Christian lyrics. We have strived to dispel the fear of using the drum; and by having it as a common feature at the camp, many of the fears about the drum are taken way. As a result, a sense of the good is placed on the drum, and many attenders feel comfortable having it played, and they even participate in the songs that are sung. These are a few examples of the areas I was looking for when analyzing the responses from the camp attenders and those participating in my questionnaire. The data collected in my study show many of the these positive aspects as factors making the Wiconi Family Camp a successful event for the past ten years.

The Rites of Passage Theme

Table 6 below illustrates the data from the responses with a re-analysis to look for a deeper theme running through the responses. As with the Brethren in Christ Overcomers data, I explored the theme of rites of passage from the responses collected from the Family Camp study. The rites of passage theme shows up in these responses in ways very similar to those of the Brethren in Christ Overcomer study. In both cases, the rites of passage theme received a significance positive response.

In analyzing the responses of the Family Camp attenders, I took the same objective approach as with the Brethren in Christ study. The following is a description of the responses. Because the world of contextual ministry is so familiar to me, I have found it difficult at times to convey to others what we are actually trying to accomplish within the Native American contextual ministry movement. The following is my attempt to expand on my understanding of contextual ministry within the Wiconi Family Camp.

Wiconi International has created a Christ-centered Native American program and has tried to reach the hearts and minds of those who come together to meet people's needs. The mini-Wiconi Wacipi Family Camp and Powwow is better than an evangelistic outreach. It is an example of taking our understanding of contextual ministry to the heart level of the Native people. The Powwow and camp attract many people who live within a faith and culture conflict. At the Family Camp, we invite them to explore what a Christian life can be as a believing Native American, and we lead them into a new internal wholeness regarding their cultural identity as Native Christians.

Richard tells a story of this wholeness found at our camp. He shares how a Cree woman doubted God's love for her because she was a Native. After hearing a lesson from Richard, she was able to say that she now believed for the first time that God fully loved her and that she was no longer ashamed.[1] Another person shared that he felt the Lord was giving back to them their Native cultural ways that the devil had stolen and had attempted to destroy, and

---

[1] Twiss, *One Church, Many Tribes*, p. 163.

Table 6: Data for Rites of Passage Theme from Wiconi Family Camp data

Theme	1	2	3	4	5	6	7	8	9	10	11	12	13	14	15	16	Total	% of Group
Enter and Exit	1	1	1	1			1	1		1			1	1			9	56%
Isolation for 3 days	1	1	1		1		1		1	1	1	1	1		1		12	75%
Feeling of freedom healing		1	1	1		1	1		1	1		1	1	1			10	62%
New Information	1	1	1	1		1	1		1	1	1		1	1	1	1	13	81%
Seeing New Identity		1	1		1	1	1	1	1		1		1			1	10	62%
Ritual and Ceremony	1	1	1	1	1	1	1	1	1	1	1	1	1	1	1	1	16	100%
Change & Transition Happen	1		1			1		1	1	1	1	1		1	1	1	11	68%
The camp changed them		1	1			1		1	1		1	1	1	1	1	1	11	68%
Dance Sweat Ceremonies	1	1	1	1	1			1	1	1		1	1	1		1	10	62%
Rites of Passage	1			1			1			1			1			1	6	37%

now he felt that he was set free to be Native again.[2] It is these types of results that have been occurring; and in every camp, we meet people that share similar stories.

The Wiconi Wacipi Family Camp takes place at Aldersgate Methodist Christian Camp in late July near Turner, Oregon, which is just southeast of Salem. Attendance at the camp varies from 250 to 300, mostly made up of Native families from the region, Native ministries leaders from across the country, and interested people from various backgrounds. The camp begins with registration at 5.00 pm on Thursday and runs until noon on Sunday. The camp is structured around a selected theme that includes Native family and community issues as well as theological topics dealing with various aspects of ministry among Native American churches. For example, last year's theme centered around contextual Christian worship, where topics are discussed and presentations made. In 2014, the theme was worship, and some of the more popular Native contextual Christian musical groups performed. These included such performers such as Cheryl Bear and Broken Walls singer Jonathan Maracle. The theme for 2015 is suicide prevention among Native communities. The presentation will be conducted by gifted practitioners in contextual ministry, and will introduce a video created by and for Native Americans called, 'Through the Pain'. The camp is situated in the tall pine forest of the northwest with a beautiful stream, where families enjoy tubing and other activities. Among the activities other than tubing down a stream, the campers can chose from a variety of events. We provide for the campers, both young and older, traditional craft making such as bead work, copper bowl making, rattle making, and hand drum making. Other activities include a water slide, rock wall climbing, ropes course, and volleyball. One of the major reasons we chose the location was for its peaceful atmosphere. Also, it is a large enough area to hold a Native American Powwow. Our Powwow is a traditional time where individuals come dressed in their cultural regalia and are able to dance to the drum beat of several drum groups from the area around Turner.

---

[2] Twiss, *One Church, Many Tribes*, p. 161-63.

Because of the lower economic level of many of the reservations in Washington and Oregon, over half of the attenders are made up of Native families that are sponsored with scholarships. We further are able to scholarship youth groups from some of the reservations, which amount to about 25 youth and leaders. As I mentioned earlier, the camp is also attended by many Native ministry leaders from several denominations, including community churches, Foursquare, Methodist, Baptist, and Assemblies of God. First-time attenders make up about one-third of the attendance each year. On many occasions we have missionaries, seminary professors, and missiologists attending our events.

One of the more traditional aspects of the camp is the building of the sweat lodges. During this time, which is one of the very first activities we conduct upon arrival at the camp grounds, I take a group of interested people and helpers to construct two complete sweat lodges. The sweat lodge is a dome shaped structure covered with canvas and tarps to keep the heat in side. The heat for the sweat lodge is made by the heating of stones in an open fire pit for several hours and then bringing them into the lodge where the sweat lodge ceremony takes place. After a teaching of the protocol involved in participating in the ceremony, those attending enter the lodge and take their seat around the circle. Water in a bucket is brought into the lodge and several dippers full of water are placed on the hot stones, creating a hot steam which adds to the cleansing nature of the spiritual ceremony, so as to have both a spiritual and physical cleansing. These sweat lodge ceremonies are conducted both morning and evening. I will explain this ritual and others in depth in the next section. The sweat lodge is similar to a fitness club sauna, which uses both heat and steam. Those who participate, experience not only a physical cleansing from the hot steam; they also receive spiritual, mental, and emotional cleansing through the prayers and open conversations in the lodge.

The usual agenda for the Family Camp runs as follows: Registration and a dinner meal on Thursday at 5.30 pm, followed by a gathering in the auditorium where we have worship performed by an invited contextual musical group. A fellowship time comes after worship. On Friday, we begin with breakfast together then gather for worship, and the first of our presentations takes us up to lunch. The afternoon is slated for family craft time and the other activities mentioned earlier. After dinner, we gather for talent night, where individuasl are invited to share their personal talents such as singing, skits, dance routines, poetry, and rap songs. Beginning Saturday morning after breakfast, we gather for another presentation, and then we prepare for the traditional Pow-wow, which lasts from noon until 10.00 pm in the evening. We wrap the weekend up with our final worship time and our last presentation. Following the last presentation the attenders say their farewells with hugs and tears.

The camp attracts Native families, Native pastors, Native and non-Native ministries leaders, youth groups from reservations, and other interested folk, both young and old. In total, our attendance for 2014 was 231. This attendance was made up of 35 individuals who were active in ministry and 128 families; 59 were part of larger groups, and 9 were members of our invited musical groups. Attendees who were active in ministry came from groups like the Brethren in Christ, YWAM, and Missionaries to the reservation in South Dakota. The families were made up of mostly families from the Northwest region, although some came from California and Texas. The two youth groups attending were a youth group from the Yakama reservation and another group of Micronesians from Pasadena, California. And finally, members of the musical group that ministered in our program came from Canada, Oregon, Alaska, and Washington. We honor all those who attend, but we do not make tribal identity a matter for our registration because many who come have no tribal heritage. We are able to put on such an extensive program at the Wiconi Family Camp because of the generous donations of many supporters. However, we must send out an appeal each year to seek for donations to make the camp happen.

Wiconi Family Camp Ministry Approach

With this type of attendance at the Wiconi Family Camp, our ministry approach needs to be a flexible and eclectic approach that is able to meet the many group and individual ministry needs. Our basic approach is very similar to the approach I used in Grand

Rapids, Michigan, where a small group of motivated church plant-
ers sought to start a ministry that looked, smelled, sounded, felt,
and tasted Native. Wiconi was designed with this same goal in
mind. With the help of many supporters and colleagues, Richard
Twiss was able to create a place that reflected the culture and
worldview of the Native people.

A few of these Native cultural aspects were worship with Native music by Native musicians, a worship center reflecting the
Long House, teaching reflecting the story-telling method, cultural
teaching with the craft time, and putting on the main event of the
Powwow. All of these and others will now be presented and explored in more depth. These are only a few of the items that I will
attempt to introduce (along with several others) to give the reader
more clarity regarding the Native ways that we have constructed
using the views of the Native American Contextual Ministry
Movement. That is, we seek to create expressions of the Christian
faith in a fully Native way. This approach stands in contrast to the
more common western Christian methods, which we are convinced are inadequate in reaching the many Native people who
have been disaffected with the western Christianity they call the
'White Man's Religion'.

When it came to the approach of the camp, many of us can
remember that founder Richard Twiss wanted to keep the structure simple. The camp started eleven years ago after coming off
of a conference series called 'Many Nations One Voice', which
was conducted in many cities across the nation. The conference
was very structured, with many speakers presenting talks on contextual ministry philosophy and methods. As this series came to a
close, Wiconi went in a new direction by creating a Family Camp.
The focus of the camp was to offer a camp where those working
tirelessly in their respective regions could come together and receive encouragement regarding the battle they were facing to promote the contextual ministry approach. Without as much structure as the conference series, this camp was to be a place to just
have fun and to build relations with others in contextual ministry.
As a result of the camp, those attending the camp became a very
tight-knit family, referring to each other as brothers and sisters
and uncles and aunties. These events are noted for offering the

attenders contextual sweat lodges, where those new to the sweat lodges could experience them in a safe and Christ-centered atmosphere. The camp went the extra step to offer a traditional Native American Powwow. The Powwow allowed attenders the opportunity to dress in their respective cultural regalia and to dance as others do at similar Powwows across the country.

Another important aspect of the camp was to make the camp affordable, so that any Native family would have the opportunity to attend. Many Native families still do not have the financial resources needed to attend, so Wiconi made available to those families scholarships from donations from a wide range of people wanting to help this event take place.

To add to my description of the various cultural events and rituals I mentioned here, I will describe the camp and follow the flow of the camp itself, progressing through the events scheduled. I will further elaborate with each aspect with noted detail.

As we describe the cultural items that we used, we must remember that this was not a very popular topic twenty years ago. With the start of Wiconi International's various events, the issue began to be looked at more seriously. Several Native American ministers and scholars began to spring up with ideas of their own. When these started to attend the Wiconi Family Camp, critical mass was formed, and the ride began. Richard makes note of this by saying,

> There are those who for various reasons do not agree with our approach ... Native people who had heard of those innovators and questioned whether they were 'correct or not', had the opportunity to watch, listen, observe and participate in the innovations presented in the formal gathering.[3]

It was nothing short of sheer genius to use the Wiconi Family Camp as a way to expose leaders to models of contextual ministry methods. If a picture is worth a thousand words, then a living example is worth ten thousand words. The Wiconi Family Camp was created to be the living laboratory where we would break open the can of creativity and produce Native American expressions of

---

[3] Twiss, 'Rescuing Theology from the Cowboys', p. 82.

Christian faith in a fully Native vernacular and expression. We made the decision that our Family Camp must offer more than just a Native American evangelical clone of a thousand other Christian camps. Instead, we chose to offer an innovative ministry that meets the needs of the people. Many of these innovations were created by utilizing Native ethnic traditions that had been viewd negatively by pastors and missionaries who had not spent the time to understand them.

We chose several ceremonies and rituals that were common among many tribal traditions. A few of these sacred ritual and ceremonies include: the sweat lodge, praying rituals with incense, Powwow dancing, singing with the hand and big drum, and playing the flute.

It is important to note that my descriptions here are not meant to be descriptions or explanations of the traditional use of these various rituals or ceremonies common to many of the tribe of North American. What follows is the description and explanation of these rituals and ceremonies as they are being re-traditionalized as contextual expressions of Christian faith. The forms and meanings of these rituals and ceremonies are my re-interpretations of them as a Native traditional and Christian practitioner. These descriptions will show how we can have the freedom to apply new meaning to old rituals and create a functional expression that can meet the needs of the Native person, needs that have never before been met when the person was presented with the gospel message. The mind set of my approach is to be a living gospel and to use words when needed. What I mean is to live out a Native American traditional lifestyle as a Believer in Christ; thus, in this way, I conduct the ceremonies and rituals without saying much in the way of interpretation or commentary to explain what I am doing. But in order to share the Gospel message more clearly to those who do not know their traditional heritage, I take the time with a group and teach and instruct them in the contextualized ritual I am performing. And I do not meaning perform as 'performance'. I mean conducting the ritual with commentary.

My explanation of the rituals is my attempt to give a window into the contextual world and into the use of these rituals and ceremonies within my ministry both at the Brethren in Christ

Overcomers treatment program and with the Wiconi Family Camp.

The Sweat Lodge: The Contextual Approach

In the summer of 2014, Wiconi conducted the Wiconi Wacipi Family Camp; and, as usual upon arriving at the Aldersgate camp, we begin the ceremony of the sweat lodge. Some may think that the important aspects of the sweat lodge ceremony consist only in those things that take place within the lodge itself. However, as with every aspect of Native people's lives, all of life is sacred. Therefore, the sweat lodge ceremony begins with the construction of the lodge and is completed with the taking down of the lodge. We arrive at the camp with all of the materials needed to construct the lodge. My creation of a contemporary approach to many of the traditional Native rituals and ceremonies begins at this point. The materials used to make the sweat lodge are different from ones used in many 'traditional' sweat lodges. I have chosen to use fabricated materials such as PVC pipe from the home improvement store, painter tarps, black heavy plastic, and even duct tape. Earlier generations of Native Americans used the best materials available to them, and I am doing the same. As in the traditional process of building the lodge, I begin by creating a dome shaped frame. I use PVC pipe for this frame, which would traditionally have been formed from various types of long and slender saplings. The covering of the lodge is made of tarps, blankets, and canvas, which in the older time would have been made of deer and bison hides. In distinction from many others who run a sweat lodge by teaching only from an already constructed lodge, I teach the sweat lodge from the ground up. Some legalistic traditional Natives might consider the materials I use wrong because they are not natural, or they are not part of the traditional way because they are fabricated. I would respond by asking, 'Where are the bison and deer hides to cover your lodge? Did you use a hardware store shovel to dig your fire pit? How about the galvanized water bucket and plastic ladle for dipping the water? How about the matches or lighter you use to light you fire? Did you cut your saplings down with a stone ax or a hardware store saw or ax?' No one today uses all-natural materials in the process of the sweat lodge. Therefore, the concept of faithfulness to the traditions seems to be somewhat relative when it comes to the use of materials.

To continue with the ceremony of the sweat lodge, using manmade materials I continue to teach the method of setting up the lodge. I pray in the name of Jesus in every aspect of its construction, blessing all of the participants helping to construct the lodge. The prayers are accompanied by the fanning of sage smoke on the participants. The use of sage smoke is common and is seen as a form of symbolic purification. The teacher explains the various parts of the construction, from the clearing of the ground where the lodge would be built to the placing of tobacco in each of the lodge poles before the pole is placed in the hole. This is done until the lodge is completed and the rocks are placed in a pit ready for setting on fire. After the lodge is finished, we gather to pray and thank those who helped build the lodge. I was taught that both men and women have a part to play in the construction of the lodge. This is the tradition that I was taught.

The following will be a brief description of the sweat lodge ceremony (service) that I conduct in a Christian contextual approach. This brief description could be explained in greater detail, but for this project I will only summarize many aspects of the ritual. The complete description of these rituals and ceremonies will be the topic of another project entitled 'The Journey of Hole in the Clouds', in which I hope to provide a complete guide for understanding the praxis of contextual ministry. I will include the critical contextualization that must be done in order for an agreed upon new function and meaning to be incorporated into a traditional ritual or ceremony.

The Contextual Sweat Lodge Ceremony
With a fully constructed lodge, leaders and attenders can now participate in the sweat lodge ceremony. The conductors of the lodge (as they are called) are the ones who do the ceremony. These leaders are made up of the contextual minsters who attend the camp. They come from many different denominational backgrounds, and each has their own style for conducting the ritual.

Outside the lodge, there are rocks heating up in a fire just to the east of the entrance to the lodge. Sage is prepared for smudging (which is the fanning of the sage smoke on the person), and there is a water bucket with ladle for pouring water on to the heated rocks once they are brought into the lodge and placed in a shallow pit in the center of the lodge.

The male participants wear shorts, and the women wear a sweat dress or a skirt and t-shirt, or they may wear shorts and t-shirt, but proper sense of modesty must be observed. While still outside, they are instructed in what they will experience, and they are smudged. Then they enter the lodge by crawling in a clockwise manner around the lodge until all participants are in. The conductor sits to the right of the doorway and the helper to the left. In my way of conducting, the helper does the leading of the songs, which are sung with a Native hand drum. The helper also receives the heated rocks from the fire, which are handed to him by the fire keeper. The fire keeper is a person who is recruited by the conductor to take care of the fire and the rocks. When everyone is in the lodge, a certain number of the rocks are brought inside. The number of rocks is determined by the conductor of the lodge. In this lodge I start with seven rocks, and an additional six are brought in to make the count thirteen, and once again three may be brought in. The first seven represent the seven instructions that I give in reference to the presence of God. The additional six bring the total to thirteen to represent the disciples and Christ. The final three are to represent the Father, Son, and Holy Spirit. The canvas is then brought down, and the next feature of the ritual begins.

Everything that has taken place up to this time conforms to the entering phase of a rite of passage. What takes place inside the lodge begins the liminal phase. Once in the lodge, the participants sit in total darkness until I light a candle. As the light of the candle dispels the darkness, I introduce the candle and its imagery as the symbolic presence of the Holy Spirit. I use Scripture to introduce this imagery. I lead the group in an opening prayer, and then we participate in a contextual song, which is a song with Christian lyrics that is sung with a Native musical instrument called the hand drum. I say 'musical instrument' to counter the many negative connotations have been placed by missionaries on Native cultural items over the years.

With these two orders of the service done, I ask the participants to take turns introducing themselves with a short prayer request for this sweat lodge ceremony. I explain that they can pray in the name of Jesus here, in contrast to many traditional sweat lodges where the name of Jesus is not permitted. I further explain that this lodge has been blessed in the name of Jesus Christ and is set apart for Christian worship and is a safe place for them to be and to pray. By using the name of Jesus Christ in my initial prayer, I set an example to them how they can pray. I then pour water on the heated rocks to create a steam, which gives the participants a physical cleansing while they are receiving spiritual cleansing. We continue these prayers until all have prayed, which usually take a 'round', that is, until we take a break in the ceremony when the flap to the lodge is opened to allow cool air to refresh the people. During the next round, I spend some time talking about whatever the Lord has placed on my heart. On the last round, I lead the communion service using a tortilla or fried bread and water from the bucket as the elements. This order of the service ends the ceremony, and the participants then exit the lodge.

The exit from the lodge ends the liminal phase, and the participants then are reintegrated into the world anew. They emerge from the dome of the lodge as a new creature, like a baby wet from the amniotic fluid of the womb. I say anew because they have never participated in a contextual sweat lodge ceremony before, and now their Christian worldview has been expanded, and a sense of freedom is given them from the use of a contextual style Native American ritual. They can now create a version of this ritual in their own ministry and tribal context with a greater sense of assurance that they are honoring Christ. They are further changed by the dispelling of the lies regarding their Native culture. Native Americans have been told that their cultural ways were evil and wrong; but through the sweat lodge, they receive permission from my many years of experience in contextual ministry to take these teachings and use them to reach the lost in their respective communities.

Contextual Praying Rituals with Incense

Incense burning is a natural part of the rituals we conduct at the Wiconi Family Camp. The various instances in which we perform the smudging (as it is called), take place in the following: blessing of the sweat lodges as they are constructed, blessing of the auditorium where we hold our meetings, during our Sunrise Ceremony with the pipe each morning, blessing of the drum before singers sing, blessing of the Powwow grounds, and personal smudging ceremony of individuals. This ritual can also take place as needed in various situations where it is desired. These rituals are similar to the biblical ceremonies when the Hebrew priests would take incense from the altar of incense, which is next to the Holy of Holies, and bless (or smudge) the Ark of the Covenant inside the Holy of Holies.

The various smudging rituals have many elements in common, but each type of ritual has its own unique components. At this point, I will share the features of the Sunrise Ceremony, the blessing of the Powwow grounds, and the personal smudging ceremony.

Contextual Sunrise Ceremony

At the Family Camp, I usually lead the Sunrise Ceremony, which takes place – as the name says – at sunrise. This ceremony can be done in several ways. The Navajo might use corn pollen and sprinkle it in a motion to the east, south, west, and the north while saying prayers for the new day. The Natives of the northern woodlands might sprinkle tobacco in the same manner and say prayers as well. The Sunrise Ceremony can also be done with pipe, depending upon the tribe and their traditional beliefs. Because I am a Christian, I conduct the ceremony with reference and prayers to Christ, whom I acknowledge as the Creator.

This rites of passage event begins as soon as I start to speak with reference to the Sunrise Ceremony. There may be several in attendance when I conduct the ceremony. We then enter the ceremony with opening the pipe bag and my cedar box where I keep the pipe and the medicines. These medicines are the sage, sweet grass, cedar, and tobacco. Incense smoke is made by setting on fire the medicines and then blowing out the flame and letting the medicine smolder in an abalone shell. This creates a smoke that is used for the blessing and for sending up prayers to the Creator. I use pure tobacco, but some traditions call for the mixing of grasses and barks with the tobacco. I was taught to use the pipe by three traditional elders, and they all used pure tobacco.

The liminal phase begins by laying out the pipe bowl, pipe stem, the shell, and the eagle feather. I then light the sage in the shell and bless each item to be used in the ceremony, including myself. After smudging, I pray over the tobacco and then give it to an assistant to distribute to the attenders. After each person has taken some of the tobacco they then put that tobacco back into a pouch from which I will retrieve it for the ceremony. At this point I put the pipe bowl and the stem together which symbolically creates the center of the universe, and God's attention is on this group gathered for early morning prayer. With the sage still smoldering, I take a pinch of the tobacco and bless it and point the pinch of tobacco in my fingers to the east placing it then into the pipe bowl. I repeat this action toward the other directions, including the ground and the sky. In doing this I am not praying to these directions and not to the spirits or the symbols some tribe place on each direction. I pray to the Creator in each direction because the Creator is in every direction that I point. A seventh direction I point to is to myself, because the Creator Jesus is also in me. Once the pipe is lit, I bless myself with the smoke from the pipe and then repeat by pointing the pipe and a puff of smoke into the air toward each direction and finish by pointing it to myself. I am the only one to smoke the pipe; I do not share it with anyone else. I close with a prayer for the people who are present, and then I dismiss the group.

At this point the liminal phase ends. Having participated in the Pipe Ceremony, the attenders enter or reintegrate again to the world with appreciation for the prayers that were symbolically sent up in the smoke to God.

Contextual Blessing of the Powwow Grounds

This ceremony is done to prepare the grounds for the day's event. Prayers said are for good weather and for safe travel for those coming to the Powwow. Furthermore, we pray that God's name will be honored at this event, that friendships will be made or re-kindled, and this piece of earth will be set apart for today to bring glory to Jesus.

I begin the ceremony by opening my cedar box and taking out the abalone shell, the sage, and the eagle fan. Standing in the middle of the Powwow circle, I light the sage to a smolder and with the eagle fan I bless myself by fanning the smoke over my head three times. After blessing myself I fan the smoke from the sage to the seven directions, as I did in the Pipe Ceremony. I walk to the eastern side of the circle where the participants will enter the Powwow grounds, and I fan the smoke to that direction and to the sky. I repeat this action to the south, west, and north. I return to the center of the Powwow ground and close with a silent prayer to Jesus. This ends the blessing, and at this the workers can then begin to set up the grounds for the Powwow. If there are workers in the area, they will come up to me for a blessing with the smoke. When all are blessed, I put out the smoke and return the items back into the cedar box.

Contextual Personal Smudging Ceremony

This ceremony is done in many cases to begin a meeting or gathering. The cedar box with the medicines of the spiritual leader are brought out. Again, the shell, sage, and eagle fan are used. I light the sage and bring it to a smolder, creating continual smoke. I then smudge myself by pulling the smoke over myself, and I render a prayer. I then face the east and move clockwise. I step in front of each person, and if the person wants to be smudged they hold up their hand, but if their hands stay on their lap, I pass on to the next person. If the person wanting to be smudged is sitting, they will normally stand, but if the person is unable to stand comfortably, I smudge them sitting down. They accept the blessing by using their hands to pull the smoke over themselves in a symbolic fashion as if they were washing themselves with the smoke. In some cases, people remove their glasses, which is fine because it was the way they were brought up. To remove the glasses is to place themselves in a more natural state as a human being. One meaning of the smudging for this type of gathering is to symbolically remove any negativity that might exist, so as not to bring it into the meeting so that the meeting might run smoothly. These negative feelings can be in many forms: resentment, guilt, disappointment, unresolved situations in their lives, and many others. Once each person is smudged, the meeting is ready to begin. I may place the shell and feather on the table or on the floor, or I may take the time to put everything away. This the basic method of conducting a smudging ceremony in a contextual way. In a smudging ceremony, those participating feel a sense of cleansing and a preparedness for the upcoming meeting. Not everyone feels the same emotions. Some may feel renewed in their spirits, and each time they partake in the ritual they feel the sense of reverence that comes only with a smudging ritual.

Native Christians and Powwow Dancing

The Church has often disapproved of Powwow dancing among the Native Americans and their communities. Missionaries and Christians from non-Native cultural backgrounds perceived Powwow dancing and other Native ways as evil. Why? Because they were different from the missionaries' ways and, therefore, were seen as suspicious, pagan, and not to be used in any way as an expression of Christian faith. If the missionaries had taken the time to investigate, they would have learned that the Powwow is mainly a social dance and takes place in community. Powwow dancing is no different than the social dances of the white missionaries' cultures. There is a joke among the Native people that goes like this: A Native person is asked, 'What is the meaning of the round dance?' In reply the Native person says, 'I will tell you the meaning of the round dance only if you tell me the meaning of the square dance'. The Powwow dancing is a social dance time. It is a way for the Native person to tell a story. In my northern traditional style of dancing, I might tell a story of a battle in war times or of a hunt for an animal for food. I act out with the various steps and arm movements the tale of the hunt or the battle. I tell in the dance the way I fought or the way I went about tracking down an animal that leads finally to the killing of the animal.

There is a rite of passage to become a dancer in the Powwow world. Some people take the time to learn it, and they enter the circle in the right way. However, some people are unaware of the protocol for becoming a dancer, and they step into the circle without taking the time to do it the proper way. Becoming a dancer begins with a desire to become a dancer. The prospective dancer must seek out a mentor to help them learn what it means to become a dancer.

The liminal phase begins once they start the journey to becoming a dancer. The liminal phase is the time spent with the mentor, making the dance regalia, learning the teachings behind the dance style, and learning the different songs that may accompany the dance. They further learn the story behind their style of dance. For example, with the jungle dress style, they learn the origin of the style, why there are metal cones used in the making of the dress, and the reason it is a prayer style of dance and a much respected style of dancing too. When all of this preparation is completed, the person is taken by the mentor to the dance circle, and permission is asked to take some time during the event to conduct the coming-out dance ceremony. A respected person is asked to speak on behalf of the dancer because speaking for oneself is seen as boasting and is a violation of the humility that is stressed. The person who speaks can praise the dancer for their positive traits and can tell of the dancer's accomplishments.

The final step to becoming a dancer in the Powwow circle is to dance. The first dance is very ceremonial, and after the new dancer has made one trip around the circle, the other dancers of the same style will join the dance. Upon the first dance, the entire community comes into the Powwow circle and welcomes the new dancer and joins them in one more dance around the circle. The liminal phase is now complete, and the person is a dancer.

The reintegration phase of the rite of passage is performed with a traditional giving of gifts. The dancer is reintegrated by giving gifts to those who attended the coming-out dance. The bestowal of honor is through the giving of gifts rather than through the receiving gifts, as might be done in a western culture. Giving gifts is our Native way of showing our appreciation to those in attendance. In the giving portion of the program, the dancer gives out gifts to the community and then to the most honored persons, which are usually the head staff people. These are the emcee, the arena director, and the head dancers. Gifts are then given to the elders and then to other members of the community. The spokesperson who was selected by the dancer closes the ceremony by thanking the Powwow committee and the attendees for allowing the dancer to have this time.

Contextual Singing with the Drum

The Native drums have been given negative connotations associated with evil spirits for far too long. I heard a story of how the drum got this negative sense. It was found in the jungles of deepest darkest somewhere, and there was evil spirit activity happening while the drum was being played. From that point on, the drum had its association of drawing up evil spirits when played. However, it was not the drum that drew the spirits into the place; rather, it was the act of asking (invoking) them to come that made them appear. The drum just happened to be playing when the spirits were invoked to come. If any other musical instrument had been playing, it then would be the instrument that is associated with evil spirit activity. My thought is this, what if the piano was being played, would that instrument also be associated with drawing up evil spirits activity?

Singing with the hand drum or the big drum can both be a part of many Native rituals and ceremonies. The hand drum is mostly an individual instrument, and the big drum is for group singing. The big drum can also be sung with a group of individuals who use their own hand drums. I have used the hand drum in ceremonies at church services, in the sweat lodge, at funerals, at weddings, and at Powwows. The big drum is sung with a group and is mostly done at Powwows to provide the music for the various dance styles. The big drum can be used in church services where it can be the only instrument for the service. For example, the Brethren in Christ Mission use the big drum as the main instrument in their Sunday worship service. There are now many contextual songs being created by contextual musicians to be sung with the big drum. There are honor songs, worship songs, flag songs, and prayer songs.

Table 7: Sacred Rituals and Ceremonies at Wiconi Family Camp

Sacred Rituals	Liminal Experience	Meaning gained from the experience
Sweat Lodge contextual way	Trust is built, new view of the ceremony, feeling of normal, program to God done, cathartic prayers are said. The heat and steam are welcomed.	Genuine prayers said in the clients' own way in English and in the Native language. The trust built in the staff opens door to healing to take place.
Praying with incense.	With the lighting of the incense, the experience forms a true connection with God. The ritual of burning incense fills a deep need.	As did our Hebrew ancestors, we also believe our prayers are ascending to God. We are not atoning for our sins but using our ancient prayer ways as authentic expression of Christian faith.
Powwow Dancing	The path to becoming a dancer is a journey of self-fulfillment. To dance allows the person a way to fully express themselves as a Native Christian.	For a Native Christian person to start the journey creates an internal relationship with the God they now believe truly loves them. There is a return to cultural way, giving them a freedom.
Sing w-Big Drum and flute	We began under protest w/ the church. We created new songs w/ Christian lyrics. We dedicated our drums and flutes to the Glory of God We created a new genre of music that meets a w/ Native believers.	After years of being denied the use of the most natural musical instrument for the Native people, finally allowed to use w/ a freedom. Native believers are now being touched deeply and heart-felt needs fulfilled. The flute gives a sense of calm and peace, creating a sacred moment.

The incorporation of these items listed in Table 7 might be seen as innovations within the Christian world and alien to the accepted expressions of faith. However, they were carefully considered as helpful adaptions to implement change. Each innovation is intended to demonstrate to the fearing Native American person that they can be redeemed from the lie about their culture and be brought back into Christ-honoring expressions of their heritage. We incorporated these rituals into the Wiconi Family Camp experience to meet the needs of Native American people for meaningful expression of Christian faith from within the long neglected/ lost traditions of their people groups. We hope to replace the western Christian traditions that have lost, or never had, meaning for First Nations people. The western traditions of Christian faith were imposed on the Natives as 'the way of doing things', and this was not bad for some people. However, for others who are now beginning to realize they never had to lose their Native identity to become Christians, experiencing contextual worship within a safe environment where experimentation is accepted and encouraged is a liberating experience. We are seeing the desire for our traditions to change to meet the needs for the future.

How can the use of Native ritual meet the needs of the Native people in this new paradigm where their rituals and ceremonies are now within the reach of becoming acceptable expressions of their faith in Jesus? When we look at the historical path of evangelism among the Native people, we see a very dismal story. The government and the Church were working toward saving the Native person and killing the Indian. As a result, many of the sacred ritual and ceremonies used by the Native people were not allowed, and the Native people were forced to accept the religion and spiritual ways of their oppressor. Thus, the sacred ways of prayer used by the Native people were replaced with the ways of another culture. Therefore, when we begin to work from this new paradigm, many avenues to presenting the Gospel of Christ are made available.

The use of the sweat lodge was a long-time ritual used by the Native people, and it had a place in their culture to relate to the spiritual world and to their communities. In the contextual approach to presenting the gospel to the Native people we now return to the familiar ritual of their ancestors. Within this approach, we can now use the same ritual, although in the contextual usage. Instead of the Native person praying to the spiritual world and the gods as they did before coming a Christian, they can now use the ritual to pray to God as known in the person of Jesus Christ. The function of the sweat lodge can remain the same, but the meanings can now be changed to meet the need for their new re-lationship with Christ.

This is where I begin as I minister to Native people at the Brethren in Christ and also at the Wiconi Family Camp. In each I have taken the liberty to create new expressions of older rituals and begin the see significant changes taking place in the lives of the Native people. The experiences of the Native people in the sweat lodge exemplify the rite of passage in which the client or camp attender enters a ritual with a liminal stage where life change can take place. Table 4 above shows that in the liminal experience, trust is built between the staff and client, a new view of the cere-mony is gained, and a feeling of normal is sensed as the ritual used by their ancestors is now used for their worship to Christ. From my experience with the clients in the sweat lodge, I noticed that when the clients prayed, a sense of cantharis happened, and the prayers said in the lodge were said with a renewed and welcomed connection with the Creator. The added heat and steam of the sweat is a welcomed experience, and there is a sense of normal. This is a way of prayer long denied them, and now is revived for their use as an expression of their Christina faith.

The experience of the clients in the sweat lodge is similar to that of the Wiconi Family Camp attenders. Both are an example of renewal of ritual that has a new place in the lives of the Native people and are now, in a different context, creating spiritual growth in those enjoying an opportunity to relate to Christ con-textually. Similarly, the use of incense in prayer ritual is making a comeback, inasmuch as it is a ritual that is part of the sweat lodge ceremony and part of the Pipe Ceremony. The responses to my questionnaire include several people who have mentioned that they feel their prayers are stronger when included with the Pipe Ceremony. When I conduct the Pipe Ceremony, I pass a bowl of tobacco for all those wishing to participate to take a pinch in their hand and pray with it and then add the tobacco to another bowl. From that bowl I will take some of the combined mixture of the returned tobacco and place it in the pipe with which I will smoke to the directions thereby sending up their prayers. The act of com-bined communal prayer brings a sense of community, knowing that prayers from the entire group are being sent to God. When I conduct the Pipe Ceremony, I act as a priest doing a pastoral prayer as during a church service. With each prayer expression, people are becoming more comfortable utilizing the incense in prayer.

Powwow dancing as a way of bringing fulfilment to the participants is growing, and more individuals are beginning the journey to become a Powwow dancer. Over the few years that we have been doing the camp, we have been honored to bring dancers into the Powwow circle for their first dance ceremony. Taking this step is a significant spiritual journey, and when done with Christ at the center, it can be the needed boost for their spiritual development. Similarly, the drum can have the same effect on those who want to use the drum as an expression of their Christian faith. We all know that singing the old hymns of our Christian faith is meaningful. However, as I have learned the new contextual songs over the years, they have become as meaningful as the old hymns that I heard as I was growing up. This has become true among those attending our events. The music is fully contextual and is sung by the attenders of the concerts. As I have stood near the stage by the performers and I have turned and watched the audience singing the lyrics of the songs, I have witnessed the powerful effect of the contextual music.

To turn this type of implementation into accepted practice was a challenge. It took much discernment and prayer, not to mention a deep understanding of these rituals themselves. We call these 'adaptive challenges' because they require experiments, new discoveries, and adjustments from numerous places in their usage within organizations, communities, and ministries.[4] We realized there was nothing salvific in these rituals or in anyone's cultural rituals, but their symbolism can be useful as understood by the indigenous users. Roberta King, notes, using her study of music with culture, that musical style is important for 'creating interest and serving as a vehicle for communication'.[5] King's conclusions regarding style can also be applied to cultural rituals, and we understand that other cultural ways can also serve as such vehicles.

---

[4] Heifetz, Linsky, and Grashow, *The Practice of Adaptive Leadership*, p. 13.
[5] Roberta R. King, *Pathways in Christian Music Communication: The Case of the Senufo of Cote D'Ivoire* (Eugene, OR: Pickwick Publications, 2009), p. 170.

These types of change and transition take a liminal period to process the implemented ritual. This liminal stage is a natural zone in which experimentations and trial and error can take place, and from that process an acceptable ritual emerges for use within the Native American community.

The Issue of Implementation of Change and Transition while in the Liminal Stage

In order for Wiconi to progress to the stage that it had reached when Richard Twiss went to be with his Lord required much change and transition with perseverance, all the while not knowing what it would eventually become. Richard Twiss and his colleagues were able to create (with the guidance of the Holy Spirit) an approach to ministry that was needed to create a preferred future for our Native communities. Creative thinkers of this caliber are few, but they are important. I am not saying that I have reached this level of innovation, but I have many of the characteristics needed to move Wiconi forward. This journey will continue to be a process, especially in the transition of the Wiconi organization. Creators are relatively few (2% to 5% of population), but we need only a few to make an exciting and stimulating world. They are the out-of-the-box thinkers, artists, inventers, and prophets.[6] I never expected be included in this group.

---

[6] Nelson and Appel, *How to Change Your Church (Without Killing It)*, p. 75.

CHAPTER 5

ANALYSIS AND COMPARISON: THEMES AND RITUAL PROCESS

The purpose for conducting the research at the Brethren in Christ Overcomers alcohol treatment program was to discover the factors that contributed to the men's recovery, and to discern whether or not contextual approaches had a significance part to play in this process. In the course of data collection, analysis, and re-analysis of the responses from the participants in the interviews, my biased approach caused me to overlook important themes during my first analysis of the data. I spent a large amount of time seeking out the contextual data, but I overlooked the other themes that were present. In the re-analysis, I began to notice several themes emerging more clearly from the data. First, the participants showed great appreciation for the program's use of Bible instruction as well as the influence of the Christian lifestyle of the staff who related to the clients while in the program. Second, the influence of rites of passage is also a theme that interweaves all of the areas of analysis, accentuating the effect of liminality on the programs. Finally, I will attempt to show how the comparison is an innovation of a contextual event taking place in each program.

In my analysis of themes from the Wiconi Family Camp ministry, I discovered that the same three themes were important to the camp participants as well. In addition, I found a new theme. During my first glance at my data analysis, I overlooked the theme of 'rites of passage', but upon a re-analysis of the same data, this theme was one that seemed to cross both programs. As noted earlier, the importance that the participants placed on the program's use of Bible instruction stuck out far more than in my initial probe into the contextual use of ritual, although it was there as well. Further, the influence of the Christian lifestyle of the staff as they related to the clients while at the program was also a prominent theme, but upon deeper analysis the theme of rites of passage was also there. It is this theme I will explore more in this comparison of the two programs the Brethren in Christ Overcomers residential treatment program and the Wiconi Family Camp. These two programs although very different share the same theme of rites of passage. The comparison of the rituals used within these two programs will be the topic of this section.

The two programs are different, but they are similar in that they relate to individuals who are seeking a more positive way of life as Native Christians. As a result of each program's emphasis on learning how to be a better person, they also provide an exploration of the rituals and ceremonies that can lead to a better understanding of who they are as individuals on this journey of life. In both programs the three noted themes are present. With the Brethren in Christ Overcomers program I discovered that the use of biblical instruction in the recovery program approach is reinforced greatly by the Christian lifestyle of the staff as they relate daily with the clients in the program. The theme of rites of passage is also present and is marked by the stages noted by Victor Turner as separation, liminal phase, and re-aggregation. Separation occurs when the clients enter the program. The three-month period of time in the program is the liminal phase. The reintegration of the clients into the world is the re-aggregation. The clients re-enter life and resume their journey as a pilgrim who has been changed by the rite of passage.

With the Wiconi Family Camp, the participants similarly enter a program with registration time (separation), spend three days at the camp (the liminal stage), and at the end of the camp they return to normal life in the world (re-aggregation), having been transformed by the rite of passage.[1] The Wiconi Family Camp was

---

[1] Roxburgh, *The Missionary Congregation, Leadership, and Liminality*, p. 27.

established from its inception based on biblical principles guided by the Holy Spirit. With the help of colleagues, Richard Twiss was able to create a unique space where lives could be changed in community with other Native people. The Wiconi Family Camp is, in practice, a place where individuals can enter and experience contextual life ways among others who fully embrace the contextual lifestyle. After three days immersed in a contextual approach, they end their liminal time with a closing ceremony. Then they re-integrate into the world as seekers on a journey as a contextual enlightened Christian. This whole experience has the marks of a rite of passage with rituals and ceremonies designed to reshape an individual's mind to embrace the contextual paradigm.

From data collected from individual and group interviews I will explore a comparison of the similarities and the differences between the Brethren in Christ Overcomers Alcohol treatment program and the Wiconi Family Camp. The result of this comparison will shed much light on the benefits of utilizing a contextual model in Christian spiritual development among Native American people. Participants gain a fuller understanding of who they are as both Native and Christian and how their participation in a contextual program can change their lives for the better.

The rituals and ceremonies to be explored will include the contextual use of the sweat lodge, the Pipe Ceremony, Powwow dancing, singing with the drum, and the smudging ritual. I emphasize the word 'contextual' because these same ceremonies and rituals are conducted in Native communities by individuals who do not profess faith in Jesus. Therefore, when I emphasize contextual, I am saying that the rituals and ceremonies I am using have been thought through prayerfully, scripturally, and theologically, utilizing critical contextualization with praxis to create new forms as a practitioner with new meanings that reflect my Christian beliefs and not those of a non-Christian practitioner.

The five rituals mentioned above are utilized in both programs (BICO and Wiconi) but do not in any way touch the many experiences and rituals that exist in the Christian non-contextual and non-Christian non-contextual worlds. With these five rituals, I will attempt to explore the comparisons between the two programs as they relate to the benefit of seeing them as rites of passage of individuals on their journey toward spiritual development.

In the section to follow I will share the comparison of data collected from individual and group interviews and some I have collected from personal conversation over the years from individuals who share a contextual awareness. These comparisons will look at similarities and differences and what I refer to as comparison and connection with the contextual worldview.

The areas of comparison will focus on three main topics: 1. the importance of biblical instruction, 2. the influence of the Christian lifestyle of the staff, and 3. the influence of the concept of rites of passage. In conjunction with this comparison, I will examine their influence as they relate to the overarching theme of sacredness and ceremony that takes place in the liminal stage in the rites of passage. One more area that I discovered from the Brethren in Christ Overcomers and the Wiconi Family Camp programs was the benefit of using cultural elements that brought a positive view of the clients' and campers' Native heritage, which enhanced self-image and self-esteem. This comparison will also be an emic[2] look at the combined data from the Brethren in Christ and the Wiconi Family Camp, which will show the usefulness of a contextual approach in personal spiritual development. The rites of passage theme was not included in my first analysis due to my preconceived preference for only the contextual approaches. However, when I allowed myself to remove the blinders and focus on the broader presence of themes in the data, I discovered this important area for my research. If I had developed my research methodology with a mind to seek broader responses, I may have found even more evidence of the use of rites of passage, a theme that seems a major part of the client's recovery.

It is this emic view of the comparison that provides the most benefit to my research and to the usefulness of contextual ministry methods. I will attempt to show how the following topics are affected by the contextual incorporation of rituals and ceremonies and the effect on the positive self-image and self-esteem of Native

---

[2] The emic approach is the analysis of cultural phenomena from the perspective of one who participates in the culture being studied, as opposed to the etic approach which is the study of culture from the perspective of the outsider.

peoples involved in these programs. I will also examine the biblical instruction that is given in conjunction with these rituals and the influence of the Christian lifestyle of the staffs at the Brethren in Christ Overcomers and Wiconi Family Camp programs. Furthermore, I will show the influence of rituals and ceremonies as they relate to the liminal stage that participants enter when they get involved in the programs. Most importantly, is the emic view that I, as an insider, will bring to the aforementioned areas of interest. These areas will be explored with a contextual emphasis.

The Contextual Sweat Lodge in Comparison

The incorporation of several rituals and practices in the sweat lodge ceremony has created an environment of relationship and the building of trust. The sweat lodge at the Brethren in Christ Overcomers treatment program has become a prominent part of the program's approach to recovery. Similarly, at the Wiconi Family Camp held in Turner, Oregon, in late July each year, the sweat lodge builds relationship and trust. The sweat lodge at the Brethren in Christ program and the Wiconi Family Camp is erected by the participants, and the traditional stories are shared regarding the origins of the sweat and its use both traditionally and contextually. The unique aspect of the Brethren in Christ and the Wiconi Family Camp is the incorporation of the Christian symbolism in dispelling the fears surrounding the sweat lodge's non-Christian use. Richard Twiss, in his doctoral dissertation titled 'Rescuing Theology from the Cowboys', states concerning the sweat lodges,

> They are considered sacred places/times of worship and intersession in the spirit of Jesus. They are conducted in exactly, or much the same way, as you would find on any reservation. They are led by spiritual leaders but contextualized to reflect faith in Jesus as the Creator. It is a time of great personal spiritual reflection and accountability, liberation, encouragement and healing.[3]

---

[3] Twiss, 'Rescuing Theology from the Cowboys', p. 85.

The sweat lodge ritual/ceremony that I conduct has many of the elements of the traditional sweat lodge. The changes that I have made to the ceremony were added as a result of several years of searching scripture for guidance and experimenting with contextual methods. The ritual uses the dome-shaped structure that is built in much the same fashion as most traditional lodges are built. I use lava rocks heated in an open fire. As noted earlier, I do not get caught up in the legalistic way a lodge should be made, and I have chosen to use PVC plumbing pipe to construct the dome-shaped frame. The reason I do this is because it is not so much what the lodge is made of, but it is the prayers that are said in the lodge that I focus on. I further do not focus on being in the darkness, which is over emphasized in a traditional lodge, but I incorporate a small candle in the lodge during the ceremony. Doing this dispels the darkness, and I share how the flame is a symbol of the Holy Spirit. By using the candle, the participants, most of whom are new to the lodge, feel more at ease; and the candle helps to create a safe environment. I have been in traditional lodges, and the sense of the darkness is an uneasy feeling. Further, I do not call upon the 'spirits' plural, but I only call upon God in the Holy Spirit to be in our presence. This too, brings a sense of a safer place for newcomers to the sweat lodge, and it enables them to participate more fully.

When conducting the lodge for those who are experienced, I make the lodge very hot, because they are more mature in the contextual ritual and accustomed to the heat. For newcomers to the lodge, I create a mild heat so as not to have anyone leave the lodge due to too much discomfort. With the newcomers, the mild heat is meant to be an introduction to the possibilities and potential of the sweat lodge as a very positive place for prayers to be shared. My main focus in the contextual sweat lodge is on prayer and not on the sweat lodge as an endurance test. There is a place for the hot sweat lodge ceremony, but for my purposes, I focus on the act of prayer and on the healing process that can take place in the lodge. Some have been threatened by traditional sweats where there is a sense of competition to endure the hot lodge. I conduct the lower heat sweat lodge in the same manner with the Overcomers Treatment Program and also with the Wiconi Family

Camp sweat lodge. In either of these two contextual sweat lodges that I conduct, I emphasize the theme of rite of passage. The sweat lodge itself is a sacred time or ritual/ceremony that can be seen as a separate rite of passage ceremony in and of itself. There is the preparation time before entering, there is the actual entering of the lodge (entering stage), the time spent in the lodge (liminal stage), the ending of the ceremony, the emerging from the sweat lodge, and the re-integrating back into the world. In this case, the sweat lodge can be seen as a rite of passage in itself. It can also be incorporated into the overall program of the Overcomers program or the Wiconi Family Camp, which as a whole can be a rite of passage as a combined event of both programs.

The rite of passage theme has emerged as central to my understanding of both the alcohol treatment program and the Family Camp, and Table 5 above illustrates some of the essential similarities and differences between the two programs. The similarities I see between the Brethren in Christ and the Wiconi Family Camp lodge include the act of ritual and ceremony that can lead to change and transition in a person's life and be a profound turning point in a person's spiritual growth as a disciple of Christ. As a liminal experience, the sweat lodge has as a part of its ritual the act of purification as the participants are prepared for the event with teaching. New information is gained by the individuals, which is one of the aspects of a rite of passage. Some of the experiences that the participants have are the purification beginning with the smudging ritual (done before the participant enters the lodge) and the purification that takes place as the person experiences the cleansing of their body by the sweat. Purification takes place both physically and spiritually.

Probably the most significant aspect of the sweat lodge ceremony that I conduct happens at the end. The Lord's Supper is celebrated at the closing of the sweat lodge ceremony in both the Overcomers program and the Wiconi Family Camp. I have conducted the contextual sweat lodge at the Overcomers for many more years than at the Wiconi Family Camp. The Overcomers program was my proving ground for the development of the contextual sweat lodge with the focus on prayer to Christ, the use of a candle, construction materials, and the use of the Lord's Supper as part of the closing of the ceremony. The time spent at the Overcomers before coming to the Family Camp made all the difference in its acceptance. When Richard Twiss heard of my method, he wanted to bring us to Wiconi as soon as possible. What Richard was able to do in promoting the concepts and the philosophical awareness of contextual methods, I was able to do in the actual practice as an insider, being both a Christian and a traditional practitioner.

The learning that takes place throughout the entire event is immense. As for the active learning taught during our programs, there are also many unspoken items taught. Both the clients at the Overcomers and the camp attenders learn so much both actively and vicariously. The vicarious learning that we try to teach are the protocols that Native people like myself know and take for granted. When a newcomer experiences the event, they engage in active learning that can only come from participation. It is in these many nuances learned that make the sweat lodge a rite of passage. One point of learning noted by participants in the interview was the presence of God that was felt while in the contextual style ritual. The second most noted point of the sweat lodge by the participants was the sense that the contextual style of sweat lodge is not as 'scary' as they had perceived it to be, and that it was an honoring way to pray to God in a fully indigenous way. Thirdly, it was noted that the presence of the sweat lodge in the context of a Christian camp was felt to be a natural part of the camp's overall structure. Their questions of whether a sweat lodge was acceptable at a Christian Native Family Camp were overcome, and the sense of it being a natural part of this camp were apparent. Many participants noted it was the presentation of the contextual sweat lodge ceremony that demonstrated the Christian freedom to incorporate Native culture as an authentic expression of the Christian faith. The clear presentation of the contextual sweat lodge removed many doubts about its proper place in a Christian setting. Further, this area of learning was carried over to the other rituals and ceremonies that are used at the Wiconi Family Camp. It also influenced the BICO participants the most.

The Pipe Ceremony in Comparison

As with the sweat lodge, there are various traditional ways to use the pipe among many tribes. In all traditions, the pipe is considered sacred and is used with the utmost humility and respect. Further, the use of the pipe in a contextual ceremony follows many of the same features found in the traditional use of the pipe. One important aspect of the use of the pipe found among many tribes is the keeping of an orthodox usage protocol. That is, if a pipe is handed down to someone in the same tribe, the ceremony taught by the pipe keeper to an apprentice must be performed to the exact tradition and protocol of the teacher. Within each tribe, they can have their own particular method of performing the Pipe Ceremony and in the way they take care of the pipe. This holds true for the new contextual Pipe Ceremony too.

I mention the above to note that the way I use the pipe in a contextual manner is to share how in this new contextual ministry approach there is a freedom to develop ritual anew. This is to call attention to the way all indigenous sacred traditions have developed over the centuries. Tradition is not static; it is dynamic, and it can change and has changed throughout history. That is, at one point within a culture there was not a certain tradition, and then at another point a new tradition was introduced. We find this true in our oral stories. The pipe or the sweat lodge ceremony was 'given' or taught to the people, showing that the ceremony did not exist before that period at which it was given. Therefore, cultures are dynamic, and new traditions can be introduced, and new rituals can be developed.

I have taken this cultural change dynamic principle and have developed a contextual Pipe Ceremony that reflects my Native American heritage and my Christian faith. I enter into this journey by seeking guidance from the Lord and the guidance of three Anishinaabe elders in the use of the pipe from their respective traditions. The Anishinaabe is the word for the people who made up the three tribes of the Great Lakes region known as the Ottawa, Potawatomi, and the Ojibway. After sharing my calling to learn the use of the pipe, each elder granted me their personal permission, not the permission of their tribe, to use the pipe as a follower of the Jesus way or the Christian way. The description of the use of the pipe in a contextual manner does not follow any strict protocol of the Anishinaabe tribes but incorporates the traditional usage, which is keeping the function of the ceremony intact while creating new meanings to those functions. It is from this basic understanding that I began to use the Pipe Ceremony as part of a sacred journey as I walk my Native traditional path and the Christian way.

With this needed introduction, I will now share from my research findings the comparison between the Brethren in Christ and the Wiconi Family Camp regarding the usage of the Pipe Ceremony in each context. At the Brethren in Christ's Overcomers alcohol treatment program, I incorporate the Pipe Ceremony as part of the client's participation in the sweat lodge ceremony that I conduct once each month during their three-month stay at the program. Each month I am invited to conduct the sweat lodge for the clients as part of their treatment program, and I also join the clients as they gather around the drum, which is positioned next to the sweat lodge. During this time, we sing several contextual songs, the last of which is a special song that is called the 'pipe loading song'. As the name indicates, it is during the pipe loading song that I prepare the pipe for the ceremony. With the beginning of the song, I open my cedar box where I keep an abalone shell to burn sage for a purification ritual and to bless the pipe, the tobacco, and all of the associated items for the ceremony. At this time, I give instruction on using the pipe contextually. I start by offering to the men the tobacco that I will use in the smoking of the pipe, and as the men take some of the tobacco, they then return the tobacco back into a separate bowl from which I will load the pipe. This is a symbolic way for them to place their prayers into the tobacco that I will use in the ceremony. As noted above in the section on the sweat lodge ceremony, I use the same ritual process for the Wiconi Family Camp participants as they prepare to enter the sweat lodge. Thus, the Pipe Ceremony ritual is conducted in the same manner in both the BICO program and the Wiconi Family Camp.

Although the ceremony remains essentially the same in both settings, the teaching component will vary according to the needs of the participants. On the one hand, at the Overcomers program, most of the men do not have a saving relationship with Jesus. They may have been brought up with some Christian understanding; but, for the most part, these men need Jesus in their lives. On the other hand, at the Wiconi Family Camp, many of those attending the camp profess faith in Jesus Christ. However, it is not unusual to have a number of camp attenders who are not believers. At Family Camp and at the Overcomers program, I always express the need for everyone to grow closer to Jesus, with the hope that the non-Christians will receive him as their Savior. At the Family Camp I further conduct what is called the Sunrise Ceremony. As was discussed earlier, the Sunrise Ceremony is an early morning Pipe Ceremony to which many from the camp are invited. It is a devotional time that enables everyone to start their day centered on Christ.

For a fuller understanding of the Pipe Ceremony in contextual ministry and its relationship to spiritual development as a sacred time of liminality, we need to look at it as a rite of passage. The beginning of the Pipe Ceremony signals the entering stage of the rite of passage, which creates a sacred space. Once the Pipe Ceremony starts, the situation of liminality begins. In the liminal state, new information is gained, and those attending open themselves to change, and they allow transition to take place in their lives. Biblical instruction is given, which offers to the participants the opportunity to grow in their spiritual lives. In many cases, both at the Overcomers and the Family Camp, a positive self-image and self-esteem start to grow in their lives.

During the Friday afternoon family time at Family Camp, I offer a special teaching time on the contextual usage of incense and the use of the Pipe Ceremony. In this class, I open the Bible and share with the class my journey toward my contextual ministry understanding. As far as I know, my class and ministry with Wiconi is unique, inasmuch as I am the only contextual leader to use the Pipe Ceremony openly as a significant aspect of ministry. It is a great honor to be called a Pipe Carrier. This is a term given to someone who is a respected person of honesty and integrity, who seeks to follow a Godly life. A Pipe carrier does not call themselves a pipe carrier, they are known to be a pipe carrier by the community.

Table 8 (below) shows how the use of ritual affects a person's life. The ritual of the Pipe Ceremony is a powerful and sacred ritual. Most men at the Overcomers understand the sacredness of the pipe, and when it is conducted they show it due respect. At the Family Camp, most new attenders to the camp do not know the sacredness of the pipe, and this why I offer the class. After eleven years of using the pipe at the camp, I have earned respect as someone who uses the pipe in a contextual manner but also as one who is a believer in Jesus Christ. Liminality is seen in the person's gaining understanding of the pipe's contextual use. The innovation that takes place in this understanding is the awareness that can actually be taken from within the Native traditional world and redeemed for the honor of our Lord Jesus Christ and used in Christian ministry in all good conscience.

Powwow Dancing in Comparison

Powwow dancing has been one of the most exciting areas of contextual ministry, mostly because it is full of flash and glitter, along with style and performance. Dancing is viewed negatively by many Christian denominations. I could never see the problem with dance, because I look at it from a different cultural perspective. Dance is a part of almost all cultures, including European cultures. A quick internet search of 'dance in Europe' will show many different styles of dance, including both folk dance and ballroom styles. It is sad that the western church as rejected this joyful tradition. We in the contextual ministry movement see the benefit of using dance in ministry. Many of the styles among indigenous peoples tell stories of the people. The Micronesian people of the south Pacific have attended the Family Camp for several years, and we have seen firsthand the beauty of the dance of these people. The dances in the Native American world vary across the North American continent. I cannot speak for other traditions, but I can speak to the dance traditions that exist within my tribal world. I personally dance the Men's Northern Traditional. As was discussed above, this style is a warrior dance where the men dancers tell the stories of battles or of hunting encounters. Within my own family, we dance several other styles. Dance is a part of my family's life, and we do not understand why anyone would want us to separate dance from our Christian life.

Powwow dancing is a form of Native American dancing that can be both competitive and social. The outfits the dancers make and wear are called regalia. People who are unfamiliar with this form of dance will often call these outfits 'costumes'. Costumes are worn to pretend to be someone else or something else. For example, during the Halloween time, children dress as goblins, ghosts, or super heroes. In the Native American world, the regalia are representative of the people and their way of life. They do not call them costumes because when these outfits are worn they signify who the dancer is. We are not pretending to be something else; we are being who we are. Therefore, when I write of the Powwow and the dancing that takes place at these events, I am speaking from a personal insider view.

I understand that some types of dance are associated with drunken celebrations, and some dances are too sexual in nature. I am not even considering these types of dancing. The ones I will only consider are those mentioned throughout many sections of scripture for rejoicing and praise. We know that the Hebrew people have dances that are still practiced with various rites of passage. Native American people have had dancing throughout their history. Every culture has good and evil in them, and dancing can be either good or evil. Some dances are for celebration and some are for evil. Within the Native American world, the majority of dances are for the good, but I admit there are evil looking dances as well.

The comparisons of dancing at the Brethren in Christ and the Wiconi Family Camp are few. At the Overcomers, I speak of Powwow dancing and present to the clients my form of the Northern traditional dancing style as an illustration of the kind of dance that is indicative of a man of respect. Because my style is a warrior dance, I share with the clients how they are warriors and how they as men must always carry themselves as warriors. I encourage them to be ready to stand up and protect their families and their communities. Unfortunately, these clients may not dance at

Powwows because of their involvement in drugs and alcohol. They are not yet examples of good warriors and have become a disgrace to their people. They are taught that a warrior is a person of honor, of respect, and a symbol of the strength of their families and tribe. Although Powwow dancing is not a part of the Overcomers program, it does have a practical side that we share with the clients. In January the Brethren in Christ Overcomers hold a traditional Powwow for the community. The Powwow is held in celebration of an alcohol and drug free lifestyle called the Overcomers Sobriety Powwow. At this event the clients are able to take part by singing with the drum, and they are able to dance when the emcee calls for an intertribal dance. During the intertribal dance, everyone can dance; and regalia is not required, so the clients can dance in jeans. With the Powwow, there is the opportunity for the clients to see the pride and respect the dancers show as they participate in the event. It is our hope at the Overcomers, that the clients will gain a sense of pride, a positive self-image, and self-esteem.

At the Wiconi Family Camp, we hold a Powwow on Saturdays starting at noon and continuing until 10.00 pm. Our Powwow dancers are mostly made up of the camp attenders, most of whom are Christian. Our event draws over six hundred people and has become a popular community event. The dancers who participate in the Powwow come from several tribes. Some dance the style of their particular tribe of the Northwest; but in the Powwow world, there are several dances styles that have taken on a Pan-tribal appeal. These dances are mostly representative of the Northern plains and woodlands tribes, and it has become acceptable for tribal members to dance these styles without being from that particular tribe.

The Powwow dance at the Overcomers and at the Wiconi Family Camp have some similarities and some major differences. As was pointed out above, many of the dancers at the camp are believers, and many have been on a journey of discovering who they are as Native Christians. The Overcomers clients, however, have lost touch with their Christian heritage if they ever had one. The Wiconi campers come from several Christian denominations, and some seek Christ without the assistance of a religious organization but find spiritual fulfilment individually or with in their family group. At the Overcomers program the men attend either voluntarily, or they are ordered by the court to attend. Some are highly encouraged to attend by their parole officers. The differences in spiritual development among the participants in each program are numerous. However, the main point in either program is the spiritual formation of all the people involved. As was discussed above, the Overcomers accomplish this through biblical instruction and through the personal relationship of the Christian lifestyle of the staff over a three-month residential program. Conversely, spiritual formation at the Family Camp takes place over a three-day span, which is much briefer than BICO's three-month program. At Family Camp, biblical instruction is delivered in the learning sessions, and these change with each year's camp. The constant at every year's camp has been the demonstration of love that is shared freely between the long-time campers and the newcomers. It is this unconditional love shared to all who come, combined with the total acceptance of everyone, that create an environment for God's love to be seen through the staff and volunteers. This love makes the camp a success each year. This similarity with the Overcomers is accredited only to our Lord Jesus to whom we give all the glory.

How does rites of passage fit into the Powwow and dancing? Dancing within the Powwow world has its own rites of passage. When I and my family first thought of dancing at the Powwow, we learned the many details and protocols that are required to become a dancer. In the Native world, as I have mentioned, there is not a divide between the secular and the sacred worlds or between the religions and the Native spiritual worlds. So, becoming a dancer begins a journey down a sacred path, and in the contextual worlds, it forms a seamless blend of the Christian and the Native traditional worlds. As an example of our situation, I will mention some of the phases we had to navigate toward becoming a dancer within the Powwow circle. We began with a desire to become dancers; therefore, we engaged in a time of prayer to Jesus Christ. It became a family matter, which led to the desire for the whole family to start the path toward becoming dancers. Each person was required to choose a dance style, and with each style came the protocol to seek out a mentor who could be the teacher and guide on this journey. Next came the selection of designs and colors for the regalia to go with the dance style that was chosen. For men, there are four major styles from which to choose: Men's traditional, Grass dancer, Chicken, and Fancy. With the women, there are the Women's traditional, jungle dress, and fancy shawl. Furthermore, if you want to use an eagle feather, you have to go through the process to order an eagle from the Department of Fish and Wildlife. Because my style requires an eagle for parts of my regalia, I had to wait until I had all the feathers needed for my style of dance. Once all the preparation is done, then a ceremony takes place at the Powwow circle during an actual Powwow. This is the point where the rite of passage concludes. The aforementioned steps constitute the entering and liminal phases of rites of passage.

I have not attempted to describe in detail the Powwow dance styles and all that is involved in learning them. I mention the variations only to show the reader the amount of learning that is required just to understand one aspect of my Native culture and the amount of critical contextualization understanding that has to take place. This contextualization is best done from an insider's view and not from the view of another cultural background. All of this is to say that rites of passage exist within the Powwow dancing world, and comparisons from the Overcomers and the Family Camp show that when these areas of our cultural world are allowed to become a part of our Christian world, change and transition take place, and ceremony is lived out in liminality. The lives of the participants are changed to a more positive view of themselves as Native people.

Singing with the Drum in Comparison

Singing with the drum is an ancient Native tradition and a natural part of the Native American world. Today there are numerous drum groups across the country who sing traditional songs of old and other groups who sing new songs. Many of these expressions of the new songs have arisen from the creation of the Native American contextual ministry movement. This new movement has inspired several musical groups to create songs specifically for the Native drum for Christian worship. Native musicians like Robert Soto from Texas and Jonathan Maracle of Canada have created many of the drum songs that have become standards that we use today. These singers have further inspired many other newer groups who are now creating even more new drum songs. These drum songs are unique in that they use the familiar rhythmic beat of the traditional drum songs combined with the Christian lyrics. These songs can take the form of what are called 'straight' songs and 'word' songs. Straight songs are made up of only vocables and chanting with the traditional Native rhythm. Word songs are songs sung with English or words of the languages of the Native people. The word songs have the same traditional rhythmic beat, although the songs incorporate Christian lyrics sung to traditional and contemporary tunes. The drum songs used with the clients at Overcomers are Christian word songs.

The Overcomers program has incorporated the use of the drum as part of the recovery program's approach and method. During the interview process for the clients to get into the Overcomers program, the clients are made aware of the program's approach. The incorporation of the drum with recovery programs is not new. But the drum songs of the Overcomers are unique because they use contextual songs with Christian lyrics. Music is a powerful medium for the expression of biblical truth and Christian theology. The songs used by the Overcomers are no different. The main difference between the experience at Overcomers and the experience at the Family Camp is that the Overcomers clients learn the songs without having ever heard them before. At the Family Camp many of the attenders are already familiar with the songs and sing as part of the opening call to worship and also at the Powwow held on Saturday. In either case, the singers and the hearers are edified, and God is glorified through the singing.

Because the songs are new to the Overcomers clients, they learn each word and its meaning along with learning to sing the songs to the drum beat. Not many people are gifted with rhythm, and this is true with the Native clients as well. Some of the men pick it up right away, and others never do, but all participate in the learning time. The time the clients spend around the drum creates close relationships with the staff and with each other. The staff and I have designed the recovery program to incorporate several cultural rituals, and the singing with the drum has been used by God in some special ways to help these Native clients break free from the destructive hold alcohol has had on them. Through the building of the client's positive Native identity, self-image, and self-esteem, the Overcomers has been able to have over 70% of the clients start a new life free of alcohol.

The healing and the sense of awe that the drum songs bring to both the Overcomers program and to the Family Camp contribute to the overall change and transition that takes place. Clients' lives are forever changed, and the Family Camp attenders learn that the drum can be seen as a God-glorifying instrument. With this new view, the songs can lead the people into a worship experience unlike any they have never seen or experienced. In either case, the sacred time created by the use of the drum and the singing is just another factor that contributes to the rites of passage theme present at both the Brethren in Christ alcohol treatment program and the Wiconi Family Camp. The new information gained is seen as an innovation to those who have never worshiped with the drum before. Innovations like these can benefit the group, even if the innovation is not a new experience to the older attenders but only for the new attender or clients.

Smudging Ritual in Comparison

The smudging ritual is where I started my contextual journey over twenty-five years ago. I had lived in two worlds for most of life, half in the Christian church world and half in my Native traditional world. As a young man, I was not allowed to be a Native in the church, and my life as a Christian was not completely welcomed in my Native world. It was during these years that I started wondering why there was such a big disconnect between the two worlds. I began to study scripture from the perspective of my Native American worldview. Before, I could only see the biblical Hebrews through the eyes of theology given to me by a western white-dominated view of scripture. With my Native worldview, however, I was able to step into a whole new world that at the time was not popular. It was like stepping away from the King James Version of the bible and daring to read other versions. I discovered that the biblical Hebrew people were like our Native American people in many ways. One was their natural earthy way of relating to God. Their world provided the roots of our Christian heritage, and they set in place many of the ways that we now relate to God. Many of the ways they chose to worship God are not used in today's church. Priestly traditions and worshiping God from within a structure first started with the tabernacle in the wilderness, and then progressed to the grand temple made of stone and precious metals. There are, of course, other ways of worshiping that are no longer used, such as sacrificing animals by draining the blood from the animal and then burning that animal on an altar. The ritual of sending smoke up to heaven as a pleasing aroma in God's nostrils is noted widely in scripture. Further, was the burning of incense. Incense burned (either animal, grain, or herbs) to God most High was honored by God, and the burning of incense to other gods was displeasing to God.

What the Bible calls the burning of incense, Native Americans refer to as the smudging rituals. As we noted above, smudging is used by Native Americans for blessings, purification, and for prayers. This ritual is used both at the Overcomers and at the Wiconi Family Camp. For instance, when the sweat lodges are built in each program, the ground and the structure to be built are blessed and prayed over with the act of smudging. Smudging is done by fanning the smoldering smoke given off by burning sage held inside an abalone shell. Smudging can be accomplished by various methods and with various herbs. The herbs used most commonly are sage, sweet grass, cedar, and tobacco. Other herbs can be used, but these are the most widely used among the Native American tribes of North America. In biblical days, the Hebrew people used incenses such as frankincense and myrrh, along with a variety of mixtures made specifically for burning. A special incense was used in the Holy of Holies to smudge the Ark of the Covenant and the Mercy Seat. This incense was kept on the Altar of Incense, which was located in the Holy Place within the Tabernacle.

One act of the smudging ritual is performed among the attenders both at the Overcomers and at the Wiconi Family Camp. A smudging can be done to people as a group, or can be done individually. Smudging can even be done to objects. When it is done to a group, the person conducting the ritual may stand either in front of the group or in the center of the group. Each person is fanned individually with the smoke from head to toe and, sometimes, both front and back. As a Christian and a practitioner in the Native American rituals, I see these smudging rituals as a rite of passage. Smudging is a sacred ritual that can be performed both at the beginning and end of larger ceremonies. Therefore, the time between these smudgings may be understood as a liminal period. The ceremony takes place during the liminal time and is the place where change and transition can happen. For those in Overcomers program, much learning occurs in the liminal phase. This ritual is considered a sacred time, and the feeling they get using the ritual as part of their recovery program toward healing. With the Wiconi Family Camp, many attenders who take part in the ritual for the very first time feel a sense of awe, and negative thoughts about the ritual are removed. They begin to appreciate the value of the ritual for personal growth. The learning gained in the liminal phase in the Native American world is sacred time and considered part of ceremony.

Much of the influence of the ritual upon the Overcomers and the attenders at the Family Camp comes from the sense of innovation that they feel is being explored by using it in a contextual way. Many of these people have heard and even seen the smudging ritual performed, but it is the use of the ritual as an expression of Christian faith that is the most meaningful in these two programs. The comparison of the smudging ritual between these two programs shows very similar outcomes. For the Overcomers, a key element is the sense of the sacred aspects of the ritual. The clients have experienced smudging in the traditional Native life, but now they are experiencing this sacred smudging ritual in the context of a Christian treatment program. Similarly, they sense the sacredness of this new form of expression of their Christian faith that was previously denied them because of fear of using a pagan ritual that may be dishonoring to God.

**Table 8: The Influence of Ritual for Participants
in BICO and WFC**

Rituals	Liminal Experience	Learning	Innovation
Sweat Lodge -- BICO -- WFC	Prayer, purification. Opportunity to participate in a prayer ritual is entered.	Presence of God is felt in the lodge. It is not as scary as thought.	This ritual can be performed contextually. A new ritual used in the Christian walk.
Pipe Ritual & bundle -- BICO -- WFC	Very sacred to clients. Sacred to attenders because if of its historical use.	Contextual usage of rituals. Greater understanding of use of rituals.	Ritual once seen as too sacred. Rituals can be changed and given new meaning.
Powwow Dance -- BICO -- WFC	Freedom of expression is observed. Freedom of expression is entered by the dancers.	Dance can be prayer. Meaning behind styles is gained and its adaptation in a contextual manner.	Christians can Powwow dance. A new dimension to the Christian dancer is opened.
Sing with Drum -BICO -WFC	Participation in Singing. It is a call to worship creating a sense of sacred space entered.	Drum songs can be learned and clients can participate Sense of Awe is felt and respect for the its use gained	Using the songs can bring healing to their lives. Drums can be used and seen as good and not bad as they have been told.
Smudging Ritual -BICO -WWFC	They enter sacred time. First timers participate. Sense of Awe.	The ritual can be used as part of their recovery program Negative thoughts are removed. It can be used personally.	The same ritual they know can be used as part of their healing. The ritual is seen as sacred with explanation of the ritual.

The world of today's Native American was created by thinking that Native culture was the problem. Thus, a faulty paradigm was set in motion to change the way of life of the Native American. Native Americans were taught by Native and non-Native church leaders alike that their cultural expressions were bad and demonic and needed to be rejected. Now, however, the contextualized approach to Native ministry opens doors to a boldness and freedom to be both fully Native and Christian. Contextual ministry did not just happen by accident; it required someone with a vision to see change happen. The contextual ministry concepts spent many years in liminality and then emerged to re-integrate the untapped potential and opportunities of both leaders and followers. However, becoming contextual often demanded a degree of disloyalty to our roots. Telling someone to step away from the non-contextual church, telling them that some of the ways of the western church are wrong, and telling missionaries that in the name of love they may have been doing damage to our Native communities closed many relational doors.[4] The move from non-contextual to contextual was a challenging process and a rite of passage. The Overcomers and the Wiconi Family Camp are two programs that have accepted the challenge to create expressions that blend the world of the Native traditional and the Christian world. These two ministries are leading the way for many others to travel, and now that many of the barriers have been removed, change has an open door for even more innovation. Programs like these are the forerunners for many more ministries that will go beyond and take contextual ministry into the future. This has been my calling from the very beginning.

---

[4] Heifetz, Linsky, and Grashow, *The Practice of Adaptive Leadership*, p. 93.

PART III

LEADERSHIP TRANSITION AND CHANGE

CHAPTER 6

WICONI – THE LEGACY OF RICHARD TWISS

How do we begin to understand change and transition within the Native American world? Since 1492 the Native American world has experienced many changes that were produced by outside forces. Into a world where life was somewhat stable, came new-comers ready to settle the land, introducing very foreign ways and bearing very foreign weapons. Native Americans at first lived among the newcomers, and soon diseases spread like wild fire across North America. It is estimated that up to 90% of the new world's inhabitants succumbed to disease. In these early contact years, groups warred against each other, battling for precious land for new white settlements. More recently, large numbers of Native American people were forcefully removed from their homes and land and relocated west of the Mississippi to reservation land. This was also compounded by the introduction of boarding schools, which were designed to remove indigenousness from the Indian with such phrases as 'save the man; kill the Indian'. Lastly, was the relocation of thousands of Native Americans from their reservations to the cities under the so-called Relocation ACT. Thus, change and transition have repeatedly altered the Native American way of life.

Mission work with Native American people has mostly taken place on the reservations where it was thought the major concen-tration of Natives reside. However, according to the 2010 census, only 22% of those people who self-identify as Native America, American Natives, or 'Multi-race Native' live on a 'Native Indian area' (reservations, traditional land, etc.) Those living outside Native areas (urban and rural) amount to 78%. Even with this information, the majority of mission work and short-term mission work continues to take place on the reservations. Throughout the Christian history of Native American mission in the Americas, the acceptance of Native people's traditional lifestyles and religion has continually faced criticism both from the government and from religious organizations.

Richard Twiss brought significant new vision and change to the Native American people and churches. Dr Twiss notes of Native Americans, 'They said they had been taught by Native and non-Native leaders alike that their culture's expressions were bad and demonic and needed to be rejected'.[1] This type of response to our cultural ways has caused many to seek a better approach to creating culturally appropriate evangelism expressions. However, those attempting new approaches have met personal and professional criticism both from within and without those respective religious denominations. Some have conceded to the pressure and have backed down from advancing in a call they have felt from God. Still, God has a remnant of followers who are answering the call to move forward in creating contextual methods.

Dr Twiss knew this situation all too well, and he knew that of those bucking the system, like myself, most are not directly involved in or employed by a denominational system. Thus, they are free to innovate without having to be concerned with ecclesial reprimand or censure, nor concerned about loss of employment, funding, or positional status.[2] Those brave individuals like Richard are why change began and it is still taking place. For years these individuals have watched as some attended church in their respective communities of faith, chaffing or gnawing at the bit because a lack of true meaningfulness in their worship in the western style of doing church. They realize that in order to be counted as believers, they were required to give up a significant part of their identity. In using western forms of worshiping and liturgy, Twiss writes,

---

[1] Twiss, 'Rescuing Theology from the Cowboys', p. 1.
[2] Twiss, 'Rescuing Theology from the Cowboys', p. 127.

However, sometimes the practice of rituals become so routine that people no longer know the meaning of the symbol, nor are they able to articulate the meaning to themselves or to outsiders. They long for the freedom to express themselves in new innovative expressions created from within their ancestral traditions that seem to connect to some collective conscious that meets a long awaited need of special connection to their creator.[3]

Those brave souls have a deep hunger to see their own community and family members feel what they are experiencing spiritually by using contextual approaches. These changes and transitions in their live have come sometimes with the loss of personal and professional relationships. Having grown up attending camp meeting every summer, I realize that these tent revivals in our region were attended only by those who wanted to follow the western traditions. Even now, they continue to attend because it fills their souls, but it is a very ineffective way to evangelize the many Native people who are disaffected by these methods of evangelism. Richard realized this problem and made a change in his ministry by stepping away from the pastorate of an all-white congregation and starting Wiconi. He saw that the majority of Native Americans needing to know Christ were more likely to experience Him through a culturally relevant and culturally appropriate approach. They long to see contextual change and transition happen. Twiss remarked that you may be doing a lot of things for God, 'But if you aren't increasing the kingdom and reaching those outside God's family and bringing in more people to become followers of Jesus' then you might as well fold up your tent and go home'.[4] These contextual approaches have not been accepted completely nor implemented fully, but Richard Twiss added to the broader awareness of innovation. Furthermore, some Native churches are developing musicological paradigms that emerge from the Native Christian communities, which serve as viable

---

[3] Twiss, 'Rescuing Theology from the Cowboys', p. 125.
[4] Richardson, *Evangelism Outside the Box*, p. 19.

biblical alternatives to the existing dominant models that came from non-Native cultures.[5]

Richard made me aware of anthropologist Malcom McFee, who has studied the levels of acculturation among the Blackfeet Indians of Northern Montana. Twiss writes of McFee,

> As a result of the study he came up with the phrase 'the 150% man' to describe a person who is mixed blood ancestry and is able to easily and freely move between his Native and white cultures effectively serving as an interpreter between the two and on behalf of both.[6]

As a leader with Wiconi, the ability to serve both my Native people and the non-Native people while living in both makes me 150% man and gives me an advantage and ability to use my gifts for God's glory more fully. This ability is similar to that of the apostle Paul, whose being a Roman citizen and a Jew gave him the freedom to move back and forth between different cultural settings. As a cultural insider in both worlds, Paul claims to 'be all things to all people' in order that he might win some (1 Cor. 9.22). A Native doing ministry to Natives is one area Richard Twiss was able to do well, but he also was aware of the issues of Native-on-Native research, as he shares in some of his writings. He notes, 'As a Native doing research among Native America people, it is my desire to produce writing informed and supported by the finding of appropriate research collecting and sharing stories – that will serve to benefit our people in a real and practical way'.[7] This too is my desire, to create a study sensitive to the cultural traditions and to the sacredness of the rituals.

Richard Twiss built an organization from the ground up and was able to lead it almost entirely by himself. Twiss was a gifted leader and was able to motivate others to join his causes. In the final years before his death, Richard sought out an equally gifted young man to mentor into leadership of the Wiconi organization. With Richard's death, his ability to mentor this person faded, and this young man soon found other employment. With a huge

---

[5] Twiss, 'Rescuing Theology from the Cowboys', p. 130.
[6] Twiss, 'Rescuing Theology from the Cowboys', p. 113.
[7] Twiss, 'Rescuing Theology from the Cowboys', p. 137.

leadership gap remaining, the leaders met and decided to have Wiconi continue as an active organization. At that meeting, I volunteered to assist with the Family Camp. Before this time, I had rarely spoken up in the decision making, but now I was taking a responsible position in the organization to make critical decisions. I was told by the staff and others involved with the camp that I would do fine, even with my soft spoken and calm attitude. I was stepping into an environment where my leadership voice would develop. During my research I read these encouraging words: '… your ability to speak from the heart is reflected just as much in the music of your voice and demeanor as it is in the particular words you say'.[8]

To find my leadership voice, I had to discover how best to use myself as an instrument to frame issues effectively, shape and tell stories purposefully, and inspire others to believe in the vision of the founder. I can relate strongly to Richard's desire to build this organization for which he had a vision that he spent his life fulfilling. The moment I received my vision from God, fulfilling that vision became the priority of my life. Whatever personal interest I had has now given way to the marching orders that I received from God. Some leaders in my situation may continue the status quo of the former leaders. Heifetz notes, 'All too often on the long road up, young leaders become servants of what is, rather than shapers of what might be'.[9] During times of transition of leadership, the incoming leaders must move within a framework of the organization, but they can also help be the catalyst for new change. What good is vision or ideas unless a new leader can help others see it?

In my case, Richard had utilized Lora and me with the Family Camp because we personified what a contextual family looked like. As the incoming leader, I will continue to be an example by embodying it and by living it out in true fashion with courage and with inspiration for other to continue to move contextual ministry into the future. This in itself is an example of the liminal phase where transition into new leadership is a process, and a process

---

[8] Heifetz, Linsky, and Grashow, *The Practice of Adaptive Leadership*, p. 269.
[9] Heifetz, Linsky, and Grashow, *The Practice of Adaptive Leadership*, p. 52.

has beginning, middle, and an end. Taking my vision into Wiconi is, as Southerland says, in 'Transition'. 'Vision is the process of following a dynamic God – which means we must keep dreaming and keep visioning to keep our churches (ministries) and personal lives from perishing (or failing).'[10]

With my new position, I had to take a long look at my own identity. As a staff member, I was entering a change and transition mode, and liminality would soon be my friend. Entering the first stages of transition, I was looking at what to change and what newness would emerge. I was putting myself in construction mode. As a new leader coming in from the outside, I had somewhat of an advantage, as I knew from my carpentry experiences that it takes more to remodel than it dies to build new. As a new leader I was in a position to help create a new Wiconi. Part of this job is to help lead Wiconi through the changes and transitions we will encounter in this liminal stage. Dan Southerland notes one distinction between change and transition. He writes, 'one of the most important differences between a change and a transition is that changes are driven to reach a goal, but transitions start with letting go of what no longer fits or is adequate to the life stage you are in'.[11]

From the beginning of my ministry journey, the way to innovation was the model of Native ministry approach that Richard Twiss had inspired in me. It has not been an easy road, but it has been a road I have chosen because of the growing disillusionment with the status quo in ministry. Heifetz states,

> For these the world needs to build new ways of being and responding beyond the current repertoires of available knowhow. What is needed from a leadership perspective are new forms of improvisational expertise, a kind of process expertise that knows prudently how to experiment with never-been-tried-before relationships, means of communication, and ways

---

[10] Dan Southerland, *Transitioning: Leading Your Church Through Change* (Grand Rapids, MI: Zondervan, 2002), p. 24.
[11] Southerland, *Transitioning: Leading Your Church Through Change*, p. 128.

of interacting that will help people develop solutions that build upon and surpass the wisdom of today's experts.[12]

This long-winded concept is one that Richard was all about, He broke the mold of traditional approaches to Native American ministry in what he would later term 'retraditionalization'. Retraditionalization is the ever-increasing understanding of reliance upon cultural beliefs, customs, and rituals as a means of overcoming problems and achieving Indian self-determination.[13]

How Transition to Contextual Ministry Happens

The transition to a contextual style of ministry or organization does not just drop in your lap, it takes a special quality, which involves listening well. Listen from your heart with curiosity and compassion, beyond judgment, to understand the sources of people's distress over a proposed initiative.[14] But how can someone from a different ethnic and cultural background make appropriate changes for a different people. As insiders, Richard and I were aware of this dilemma of walking in their shoes, seeing with their eyes and feeling with the heart as a Native Christian. The movement to an acceptance of contextual methods has been a process, it had a beginning with innovators, then early adaptors as noted from Diffusion of Innovation theory, and is now on the down side of Roger's bell cure to the place where late adaptors are making their way into the ranks of the contextual ministry paradigm. But they too, need to be sensitive to the needs of ministries effectively reaching postmodern people realizing that felt needs are very important. There are needs for belonging, relationship, community, identity, spirualty, and an experience of the transcendent.[15]

These human needs are similar to most of all humankind but within the Native American world there is a unique distinction having to do with their spiritual lives. Paul Hiebert makes an

---

[12] Heifetz, Linsky, and Grashow, *The Practice of Adaptive Leadership*, pp. 2-3.
[13] Twiss, 'Rescuing Theology from the Cowboys', p. 38.
[14] Heifetz, Linsky, and Grashow, *The Practice of Adaptive Leadership*, p. 266.
[15] Richardson, *Evangelism Outside the Box*, p. 87.

observation on how cultures and religions are closer in some groups than others. 'In traditional cultures it is hard to draw a sharp line between religious and non-religious practices. In many societies religion is a core of the culture and permeates all of life.'[16] Many tribes as with my own Potawatomi tribe do not distinctly show division between the sacred (religion) and the secular (everyday). So as insiders living in two worlds at the sometime Richard had to balance these worlds so as not to interfere with those who do not understand our beliefs. This had led me to step back and ponder how research has been conducted among Native peoples over the years. As insiders we find it hard to treat Native people as research objects and people as merely data. To do research with the Brethren in Christ Overcomers alcohol treatment program, with the organization and staff relations with Wiconi, and as a Native American person stepping into leadership it's personal and it can be seen very dehumanizing. Native people have over the years been studied over and over. Every generation of non-Native people want to know more about Native people. The fascination with Native people is still there and even more as the contextual ministries are growing. With interview and questionnaires, I struggled to handle this project's research as raw empirical date used to fulfil the requirements of a degree. This not a new issue among Native Indigenous peoples involved in research. Native researcher Beatrice Medicine has written on these concerns, and she notes, 'Native populations are wary of others' interpretations of their behaviors, even when they are dealing with one of their own'.[17]

From Richard to the Future

This study is my attempt to look at rites of passage (transition, change, and liminality) and the processes that take place within various situations in our lives. I will look at the process of change and transition and the place of liminality in individuals and organizations as they attempt to move forward. It will also look at the

---

[16] Paul G. Hiebert, *Anthropological Insights for Missionaries* (Grand Rapids, MI: Baker Academic, 1986), p. 184.

[17] Beatrice Medicine and Sue-Ellen Jacobs, *Learning to Be an Anthropologist and Remaining Native: Selected Writings* (Champaign, IL: University of Illinois Press, 2001), p. 5.

rituals and ceremonies of change, transition, and liminality as an innovation that leads to creating new directions.

Richard Twiss' passing left a large gap in leadership in the Wiconi organization; and, as a result, decisions had to be made as to its future. This transition point has led us into a neutral state where transition and change are ripe. Transition's 'function is to close out one phase, reorient and renew people in that time we are calling the neutral zone, and carry people into the new way of doing and being that is the beginning of the next stage'.[18] But what would the next stage be?

For one year we stayed in a ritual state of limbo by taking what is referred to in Native American traditions as a time of mourning for the death of a loved one. The time period of mourning is a year from time of death, but it can last for several years. In January 2014, one year after Richard's death, the current staff and board members, friends of Wiconi, and key leaders gathered over a full weekend to deliberate concerning God's leading for the continuation of the main Wiconi ministries. We were encouraged from scripture, affirming that we do believe God is able to do immeasurably more than all we ask or imagine, according to his power that is at work within us. We agreed to trust God and not to limit him (Eph. 3.20). We understood that there were many changes and transitions ahead, and some that we had already gone through. We knew our future would have many more challenges. William Bridges notes, '… the idea that the past, which people are likely to idealize during an ending, was itself a time – and even the product – of change. Their past was started in unstable times. But became the "good old days".'[19] Thus endings, neutral zones, and beginnings are an ongoing aspect of an organization's life cycle. Wiconi began as the brain child of Richard Twiss, who took a stand and dreamed of an organization that could make a great impact in the lives of Native American communities and families in what he called 'creating a preferred future'. William Bridges has mapped this process and explains that 'renewal must begin with redreaming the dream on which the organization is based. It will involve

---

[18] Bridges, *Managing Transitions: Making the Most of Change*, p. 82.
[19] Bridges, *Managing Transitions: Making the Most of Change*, p. 36.

getting a new central idea around which to build the organization's activities and structure.'[20] The organizational transition Wiconi went through was monitored and planned with both the past and the future in mind.

Although it was Richard Twiss' death that accelerated change and transition, looking for new leadership required thoughtful planning. Through the year after Richard's death, I spoke to several people in Wiconi leadership and shared my intent to help in most any way to see Wiconi International continue into the future. I had planned with the staff to help the Wiconi Family Camp to take place as scheduled that first year. During the course of this planning my secular job came to an erupt end, leaving me unemployed and in search of new employment. As always has happened in my life, an ending of one life situation clears the ground for a new beginning.

In my story, I did little on my part, except to make myself available to be used by God. As a result, the Wiconi board offered me a staff position as the Wiconi Family Camp Director and the next year asked me to become the Director of Wiconi. Some transitions are like this and are not planned; they just happen. Now here I am, the Director of Wiconi. I have been given a great opportunity. Sometimes you can work hard to create opportunities, but at other times everything is just given to you, just as I was given the opportunity to bring myself and talents to the future of Wiconi. I was to be a part of a growing contextual movement formed by a generation of young Native American ministry leaders who were becoming increasingly disappointed with the ineffectiveness of the western character of Christianity in which we had been trained.

Wiconi is in the midst of change and transition as a result of the loss of Richard. He was the reason so many of us thrived in ministry. It was his leadership and vision that gave the inspiration and just what the Native American contextual movement needed. Although it did not start with ease, Wiconi soon became the hub on which we centered much of our own ministries. Now we begin a new chapter in contextual ministry. With the ending, a new

---

[20] Bridges, *Managing Transitions: Making the Most of Change*, p. 88.

beginning arises, as William Bridges tells us. Native people over the years have gone through many such endings and beginnings. When one of these transitions happens, we say, 'our circle has been broken and needs to mended'. Native American life ways and identity are contextually being stressed to survive. We regain much of the loss by redefining and reshaping what is left of our world. As was noted above Twiss called this process of adaption 'retraditionalization'.[21]

Part of the process of bringing us into the future will entail a season of transition and change, in which we experiment with methods we believe will bring about spiritual development in the Native people to which we minister. Working within our current framework, we have a history and legacy to uphold, but we also must show that we are progressive and willing and able to face a new future. 'We need to create contexts for the Holy Spirit to awaken people to their spiritual longing and begin to see Jesus as the possible satisfier of these longings.'[22] I believe this is a step that may be the biggest missing link in our evangelistic strategy. Knowing this situation and my desire to move more toward discipleship and spiritual development in our structure, we need to work toward making staff and colleagues better prepared to face the new future. Samuel Chand and Cecil Murphey make this remark: 'My point is that a future church (ministry) would have acknowledged the transition before it became readily apparent to everyone, and it also would have figured out what it could do about the situation.'[23] The situation includes people who have been working with Wiconi for years. This group have a loyalty to Richard Twiss and his vision that needs to be nurtured and maintained through sensitive communization. 'Refashioning loyalties is some of the toughest work in life. But to abandon loyalties is too far to go. People hold on to ideas as a way of holding on to the person who taught them the ideas.'[24] And in our situation, this person is Richard Twiss. So, to move through this liminal stage,

---

[21] Twiss, 'Rescuing Theology from the Cowboys', p. 35.
[22] Richardson, *Evangelism Outside the Box*, p. 60.
[23] Samuel R. Chand and Cecil B. Murphey, *Futuring: Leading Your Church Into Tomorrow* (Grand Rapids, MI: Baker Books, 2002), p. 52.
[24] Heifetz, Linsky, and Grashow, *The Practice of Adaptive Leadership*, p. 28.

especially when our future will include change, we must heed the advice of William Bridges. He argues that we must see 'innovations as developments that build on the past and help to realize its potential'.[25] This way we can honor the past for what it accomplished and still build Richard Twiss' preferred future. Innovation will be a part of creating this preferred future, and the diffusion of these innovations involves relations with people that can lead to change. Rogers speaks of interpersonal channels to help create change in behavior. He says, 'Interpersonal channels are more effective in forming and changing attitudes toward a new idea and thus in influencing the decision to adapt or reject a new idea'.[26] With the Wiconi family, this will involve creating new loyalties. 'To lead adaptive change, you have to refashion loyalties, that is, having a conversation both in your heart and in person with people to whom you have loyalties.'[27] By having trusting relationships to begin with is a plus when starting a change process. This will be the story for Wiconi for several years while new loyalties are built under my leadership.

Innovations and Influence

There are many dynamics interacting in any change and transition process. As with the initial research for this project, the clients at the Brethren in Christ Overcomers alcohol treatment program have many of the same situations involved in the clients and staff at the program. Change and transition and liminality are at work in most any situation, and in these situations, progress is happening as process. As with the clients at the Brethren in Christ, the staff at the Wiconi organization, and the leadership transition, the influence of the innovators creates the future.

There is a process that each of these situations follows, and it has to do with Allen Graft's chart illustrating acceptance and rejection. Allen Graft notes several steps from rejection of ideas to acceptance of those ideas in most situational changes. He notes

---

[25] Bridges, *Managing Transitions: Making the Most of Change*, p. 53.
[26] Everett Rogers, *Diffusion of Innovations* (New York: Free Press, 2010), p. 36.
[27] Heifetz, Linsky, and Grashow, *The Practice of Adaptive Leadership*, p. 264.

the following series of stages: 1. a state of confusion and denying, 2. a feeling of anger and fighting back, 3. the sense of feeling sad or numb, 4. a progressive natural allowing of a change of transition, 5. a willing acceptance of changes, and 6. a solid commitment to the implemented changes.

Figure 1: Allen Graft's Process of Acceptance/Rejection[28]

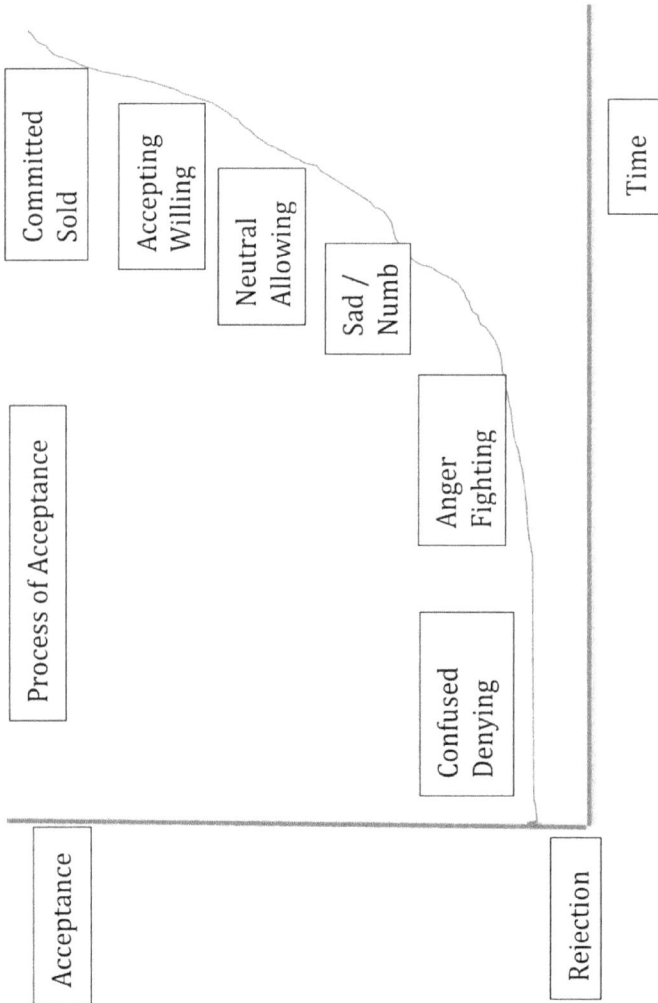

---

[28] Nelson and Appel, *How to Change Your Church (Without Killing It)*, p. 241.

This graph is similar to Everett Rogers' bell curve graph in *Diffusion of Innovations*, but Graft's chart seems to focus more on the individual while Rogers' chart looks at a group's acceptance of an innovation. Acceptance or rejection of any change is rooted in a people's or a group's fears of the unfamiliar. Richard Twiss notes how we approach the Wiconi Family Camp. He states,

> In contextual gatherings such as these – though specifically organized for the Native person – non-Native believers find themselves equally encouraged and strengthened spiritually. Old fears are dispelled and new understandings open their heart to the life of Jesus in ways previously rejected.[29]

Our gathering is unique, in that we are able to assist individuals who are in their own liminal stages of cultural understanding. Likewise, we who are at a much higher level of contextual understanding are in a liminal stage in that we are in the activity of creating a unique environment. When people are in a neutral zone in their journey, they are more likely to accept contextualization, because the neutral zone automatically puts people into unique situations, making the time ripe for creative opportunities.[30] We have found that we can capitalize on the confusion by encouraging attenders to innovate. Similarly, within the Wiconi organization, we can use this time of transition and confusion as a time ripe for opportunities to innovate. Instead of looking at confusion, leadership takes advantage and can take the group step-by-step down the road. Most everything I have referenced thus far is stated in Lingenfelter's *Leading Cross-Culturally*. He notes that innovation requires the following: 1. Build trust within a relational community, 2. Define a compelling vision for life, 3. Step out ahead, 4. Call others to follow, and 5. Empower those who follow.[31]

William Bridges has thought through this area of transition and change and the neutral zone between the end and the beginning. So has Robert Quinn, who writes,

---

[29] Richard Twiss, *Rescuing the Gospel from the Cowboys: A Native American Expression of the Jesus Way* (Downers Grove, IL: InterVarsity Press, 2015), p. 225. This is the published version of Twiss' dissertation.

[30] Bridges, *Managing Transitions: Making the Most of Change*, p. 43.

[31] Lingenfelter, *Leading Cross-Culturally*, pp. 16-17.

Few of us think about the pain suffered by those who dare to serve with both their heads and their hearts. Leadership is nothing like it appears to those who follow. I suspect that such people have discovered that the pain of leadership is exceeded only by the pain of lost potential.[32]

God has opened a door for me to step into ministry and has provided the means to accomplish his work. You would think someone would jump eagerly at such an opportunity. I thought I would, but I took the time necessary to make a major decision. Lora and I took the time to process the offer with reflection and prayer. Major transition and change like this are the ending of a way of life and the beginning of another. Reggie McNeal explains: 'This takes time and reflection. However, I am convinced that the most effective leaders are those who take time to ponder what God is up to in their own lives.'[33] There are many individuals like myself, working for the Lord from many backgrounds, ethnicities, and social standings; and all in their own special way, they sense God's calling upon their lives. I have had the opportunity to meet many of the Lord's workers, and I am convinced that he truly loves diversity; therefore, I am joining good company. Plueddemann says the following concerning our unique identities, 'Three things that shape us are our common human nature, the culture that fashioned us, and individual personalities that make us unique', but these things that shape us also give us many differences as well.[34] Our callings come to all of us in ministry in different ways. Those of us who have had a calling always seek confirmation for our calling because we want to serve Jesus Christ fully and wholeheartily. Plueddemann comments further, saying, 'Leadership is the gift of the Holy Spirit. We can be sure that the Holy Spirit gives the gift of leadership whenever and wherever it is needed.'[35] He gives the gift to evangelists, teachers, preachers, and even to carpenters hired as new Wiconi staff.

---

[32] Robert E. Quinn, *Deep Change: Discovering the Leader Within* (San Francisco: Jossey-Bass, 1996), p. 177.

[33] Reggie McNeal, *A Work of Heart: Understanding How God Shapes Spiritual Leaders* (San Francisco, CA: Jossey Bass, 2011), p. xv.

[34] Lingenfelter, *Leading Cross-Culturally*, p. 72.

[35] Lingenfelter, *Leading Cross-Culturally*, p. 125.

When I look at the way the contextual ministry movement has spread and how I have grown in my understanding, I realize the process I had to travel through. Similarly, everyone walking this path has traveled a pattern developed and analyzed by Everett Rogers in his concept of the 'diffusion of innovations'.[36] William Bridges illustrated the concept as running in a race. He explains it this way,

> like a road race, the front runners take off and lead the way once they hear the gun, secondly the next fastest runners move when the front pack begins to move. The word gets back to the middle of the pack and they begin to run, first slowly then picking up the pace. Finally, the rest of the slower runners get in the race when they hear a rumor coming back through the crowd that the race has started.[37]

Figure 2: Everett Rogers' bell curve diagram[38]

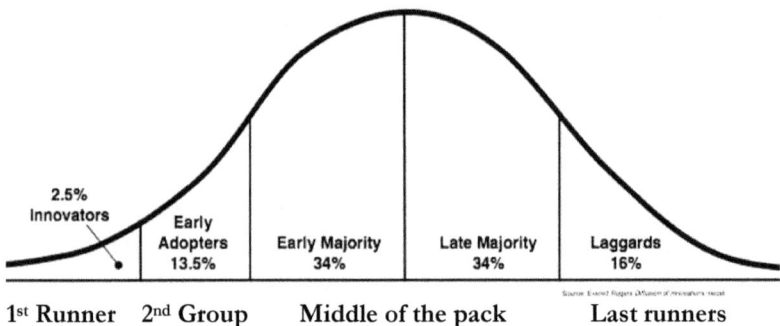

2.5% Innovators	Early Adopters 13.5%	Early Majority 34%	Late Majority 34%	Laggards 16%
1st Runner	**2nd Group**	**Middle of the pack**		**Last runners**

Source: Everett Rogers Diffusion of Innovations model

Beginnings are part of the process I have been working on thus far, and they are for me rituals and ceremonies (rites of passage). I have mentioned three approaches to seeing transition and change and the liminal stage. From my perspective, coming into leadership with Wiconi was something I had not planned, but it was something I was preparing for through all of my life circumstances. Starting this new path is just another ending/beginning, neutral zone or liminal period, and beginning/ending that I am

---

[36] Rogers, *Diffusion of Innovations*.
[37] Bridges, *Managing Transitions: Making the Most of Change*, p. 65.
[38] Rogers, *Diffusion of Innovations*, pp. 258-62.

prepared to step into. William Bridges explains starts and beginnings as follows:

> Starts take place on a schedule as a result of decisions, they are signaled by announcements. Beginnings, on the other hand, are final phases of this organic process that we call 'transition,' and their timing is not set by dates written on a schedule. Beginnings follow the timing of mind and heart.[39]

This new life direction is causing me to look at life more fully. This year I will be turning 58, and the important things in life have been on my mind more and more, especially as they relate to my new life work with Wiconi (besides my family that really matter).

I must say something concerning a dream I had while pondering the changes and the transitions of entering ministry with Wiconi. What was my place in Wiconi, and what would it mean to carry on the vision of Richard? In the dream I met with Richard, and we chatted for a while. I finally asked him, 'What should I do? How can I honor your life and legacy through my life as I help continue your life's work with Wiconi?' He sat for a while and stared into the sky, and then said these words to me: 'Case, all of life is a blessing from God, make your family life a priority, because your children will grow up so fast and be on their own before you know it; don't take life so seriously, but take God very seriously. Enjoy your time working for the Lord, and have some fun along the way too. Treat people with respect.'

---

[39] Bridges, *Managing Transitions: Making the Most of Change*, p. 58.

CHAPTER 7

THE LIMINAL PHASE OF TRANSITION

The courage to enter the change process is generated by the belief that we will come out on the other end different from the way we entered. We want to believe that changes will be made that will affect not only our lives but the lives of many more. 'Like any transition, this one could bring you out in a better place. You could well look back at it years hence and marvel at your inability to understand just what was going on.'[1]

This time of change and transition will be only one chapter in your life. Throughout my life chapters, I have gone through some changes that came easily and other changes that required enormous amounts of work. Some examples of changes in my life include being born, becoming a teenager, getting my driver's license, graduating high school, my first steady job, entering college and graduating, joining the military to become a soldier, getting married, having a baby, becoming a Powwow dancer, and completing a vision quest. The most recent chapter of my life that has included serious change and transition began with my appointment to the staff with Wiconi, followed by leaving my employment as a carpenter and becoming the director of Wiconi International. When I look back, I hope to marvel at the transition and changes and the liminal period I had to go through.

The Brethren in Christ Mission also had to make some critical changes in order to get to where they are today, and some of the

---

[1] Bridges, *Managing Transitions: Making Sense of Life's Changes*, p. 72.

changes were very challenging. Before they could become a unique treatment program with a high success rate, they had to go through a major rite of passage that consisted of adopting a humble yet bold attitude toward change.

Some ministries, both in churches and in treatment programs, display an arrogant attitude toward the rightness of their methods and their leadership. It is easy for leaders and followers to be seduced by the illusion that they have the right form for God's work, and they begin to trust their form and system rather than trusting God.[2]

In the ministry world that Richard Twiss had to negotiate through the years, there were some very hard challenges to overcome. For one, there were a few stubborn individuals who made contextual ministry change very difficult for him, only because their view conflicted with his. He also encountered the attitude that current methods are infallible, and they are the only way to do ministry properly. This attitude is similar to the attitude we see when some people strongly believe one version of the Bible is the only 'right' version for the church to use. 'Most of the time, before a change occurs that will become fruitful, we must allow the death of something else. Hanging on to outdated ministry and religious traditions because of the meanings they used to provide can be a morbid practice.'[3] In the case of the Hebrew people, they had to let go of the influences of Egypt before they could move to the promise land. In the case of the Brethren in Christ Mission, they had to let go of the past influences of the liturgy and ministry methods of their denomination. The Brethren in Christ Mission was looking for ways that would better reach and help the Native Americans to accept the gospel and bring men out of alcoholism, and they realized that the older methods and approaches were not producing the needed results.

---

[2] Lingenfelter, *Transforming Culture*, p. 101.
[3] Nelson and Appel, *How to Change Your Church (Without Killing It)*, p. 65.

Liminality and Contextualization

All of these aforementioned cases and situations require a process of entering change, a time in liminality, and a transition back into the world. To become a contextual ministry, a church or program requires the development of an understanding of different methods. Darrel Whiteman gives the following statement on contextualization. He says,

> contextualization means to develop unique, locally-informed contextual expressions of the gospel. The result will be that the gospel itself is understood in ways the universal church has neither experienced nor understood before. This expands the insider churches' understanding of the kingdom of the Creator.[4]

When these types of expressions are approved for experimentation and then implementation, they will require a time for processing the changes. This has been one of the major issues related to contextual ministry. The issue, however, is not only about the rightness of a change, but it is also about how the change will affect the spiritual development of individuals. Native minister Craig Smith of the Christian and Missionary Alliance Church states, 'I believe the best person to decide how a traditional person conforms his life to biblical principles is the traditionalist himself under the guidance of the Holy Spirit'.[5] Unlike Craig Smith, however, I believe it is the indigenous innovator and not the traditional person who can best make the decisions to use contextual approaches.

The most critical time to make the transition and change is during the liminal phase. In many ways, making change in the liminal phase hinges on your commitment to the cause. In the between time of a rite of passage, the door to experiment opens up. In my experience, I felt a strong desire to be creative and to experiment with many possible ways to contextualize. Sometimes

---

[4] Darrell L. Whiteman, *Anthropology and Mission: The Incarnational Connection* (Chicago, IL: CCGM Publishing, 2003), pp. 2-4.

[5] C.S. Smith and Bill McCartney, *Whiteman's Gospel* (Winnipeg, Manitoba: Intertribal Christian Communications, 1998), p. 126.

this would mean speaking directly to the issues, not only in regard to my personal ministry approach but also in regard to many who were just coming into the realization of the legitimate usage for contextual methods in their own ministries.

In the process of understanding for new 'realizers', your 'intervention is evidence of your commitment to your purposes, but it is not your final word on how to get from here to there'.[6] I explored many possibilities and usually was experimenting with more than one at the same time to find those that worked the best. When experimenting with a Potawatomi ritual or ceremony, I also was thinking how that approach might work in another Native tribe's cultural setting and context. Through the rites of passage process, I realized it takes a special type of person to lead change. It takes someone who has the vision well established in their own mind and feels an urgency to see a process developed that can lead to change. Richardson notes, 'There is certainly a need for prophets who call us back to the ancient ways. But there is also great need for evangelists who will translate core values into new practices that will resonate with and reach pre-Christian people.'[7]

You Cannot Not Change

'The word "change" means to cause to turn or pass from one state to another, to vary in form or essence, to alter or make different.'[8] The ancients realized this and developed rituals to show people a way to move with purpose from one stage to another. So, whether the change is dealing with the age of a person (as in a puberty rite), social status change, or even in the transition to the world of the dead, there was a way to cope with the change through ceremony. At the Brethren in Christ Mission, the aim is to work with Native men who are trapped within the throes of alcohol and drugs addiction. As a rite of passage, they have to start the program then enter a re-learning stage in a neutral zone or liminality phase which prepares them for an ending or reintegration into

---

[6] Heifetz, Linsky, and Grashow, *The Practice of Adaptive Leadership*, p. 277.
[7] Richardson, *Evangelism Outside the Box*, p. 25.
[8] Nelson and Appel, *How to Change Your Church (Without Killing It)*, p. xiv.

society. The rite of passage enables them to live at a new level in society without addiction problems.

Through the rite of passage of the Overcomers program, those individuals have broken away from the default setting that alcohol and drugs had produced. Through years of usage from day to day, defaults are established that require a de-programing time which takes place at the Brethren in Christ program. 'Changing behavior at the level of default settings requires new insight and ongoing practice, practice, practice.'[9]

The process is similar to the way a habit is changed or created. It is said that it can take from 20 to 40 days to change or make a habit. We all have habits, some are good and necessary, but others are harmful and destructive for us. Changing these habits or default settings is to change the picture of reality that lies in the mind of the individual. The clients at the Overcomers program are controlled by a destructive image of reality, and the Brethren in Christ program helps the clients to see a new reality, which consists of a life without drugs and alcohol. The clients are changed through the influence of new ideas or 'innovations'. These new ways may have been known but never developed or lost from view by a drug and alcohol lifestyle. The Brethren in Christ program is a liminal period associated with the separation of the person from community life, the giving of new knowledge, and the creating of new identity and habits and new picture of life without alcohol. Bridges observes that the

> picture in people's heads is the reality they live by, and one of the losses that takes place during the ending phase of the transition is that the old picture – the mental image of how and why things are the way they are – falls apart. Much of the pain of the neutral zone comes from the fact that is a time without a viable personal or organizational life picture.[10]

[9] Parks, *Leadership Can Be Taught*, p. 86.
[10] Bridges, *Managing Transitions: Making the Most of Change*, p. 64.

The Change Solution Lies in the People

A person's mental picture of reality drives their behavior, and the remedy for destructive behavior begins with changing the person's picture of reality. The method used by the Brethren in Christ program has proven to be effective. They look at the clients in the following manner, 'Because the problem lies in people, the solution lies in them, too. So the work of addressing an adaptive challenge must be done by the people connected to the problem.'[11] Like a medicine man or shaman who knows how to treat the problem in people, they focus on the answer to the problem not the symptoms. Much of modern medicine works on the symptoms of a problem, but the way to treat a problem is to work with the person in the psychological no-man's land between the old reality and new one. It is the limbo between the old sense of identity and the new. It is the time when the old way of living (or doing things) is gone but the new way does not feel comfortable yet. It is a time when it is not clear who you are or what is real. 'Coming out of transition and making a new beginning, this is when people develop the new identity, experience the new energy, and discover the new sense of purpose that make change begin to work.'[12]

To Enter the Liminal Door

Within the transition, change and liminality is the point when clients desire to change even though the longing to drink continues to loom over them. At various points in the clients' program, they tap into their true desire to change, and this desire can be a continual motivation for them to redeem their lives. When this happens, it is an awakening to that fact that change could actually happen. Unfortunately, some never realize this notion and never make the break with alcohol. Those who enter the program unwillingly or unwittingly find it very hard to admit that a new beginning and a new phase of their lives might be at hand or even be possible.[13]

---

[11] Heifetz, Linsky, and Grashow, *The Practice of Adaptive Leadership*, p. 74.
[12] Bridges, *Managing Transitions: Making the Most of Change*, p. 5.
[13] Bridges, *Managing Transitions: Making Sense of Life's Changes*, p. 9.

Within the liminal environment, clients rediscover a healthy view of life that had been obscured by their addictions, and an awakening takes place within them. This is what innovation is all about. It is not a grandiose idea never known before (like the introduction of the wheel). It can be basic ideas explained to the unknowing person as an innovation, and this new awareness affects the entire group in the program. 'Diffusion of innovation', as explained by Everett Rogers, is the process by which an innovation is communicated through certain channels over time among members of a social system.[14] The clients at the Brethren in Christ are a living example of just such a social system.

**Table 9: Structure of the Ritual Process for
Change and Transition**

SEPARATION: Clients are interviewed for entry to the Overcomers. They enter the program away from friends and family. The program has rules. No drugs or alcohol are available.
LIMINALITY: Start with the realization that life as they knew it has now changed. Their bodies start to go through changes. They start to eat regular meals. Classes begin in Bible, computer, finance, relationships. Innovations are made with new information. Prayer in the contextual way and the first Sweat lodge. Clients observe the Christian lifestyle of the staff. Clients attend The Mission's church service on Sunday afternoon. Field trips are taken to cultural sites and visits to local churches.
REINTEGRATION: Week prior to graduation one last Sweat lodge is held. Special Pipe Ceremony done to bless the clients. Family and Friend attend the Graduation. Clients prepare to leave and step back into their communities

---

[14] Rogers, *Diffusion of Innovations*, p. 35.

CHAPTER 8

CURRENT REALITIES AND ADAPTIVE WORK FOR THE FUTURE

My personal approach to creating change in this paradigm of ministry was to take advantage of the boldness that God had given to me and address the need to create new methods, approaches, and styles of ministry. I was not certain that this was the right way to proceed, but I knew we had to do something, and I realized that whatever we did should be treated as an experiment. All the while, I kept in mind Rogers' theories regarding the diffusion of innovation. He states, 'Diffusion has a special character because of the newness of the idea in the message content. Thus, some degree of uncertainly and perceived risk is involved in the diffusion process.'[1]

Prior to becoming the director of Wiconi, I ministered as a weekend warrior. Monday through Friday I worked a full-time job as a carpenter, and on the weekends I ministered. Over the years, I have attempted to challenge myself to enter full-time ministry. Whenever I thought I was ready to make that move, I would sense the Holy Spirit leading me to be patient. Patience has been hard for me, yet with the help of Lora, I held off until this opportunity came. This is, after all, a new chapter in our life that is just beginning. I have not become someone else; I am still me, and what you see is what you get, although I am very willing to learn and grow.

---

[1] Rogers, *Diffusion of Innovations*, p. 35.

We have a huge challenge ahead, and I want to make sure I am motivated biblically to reach out to the lost. This is what keeps me focused, and I believe it will be the key to keeping me going when things get tough.

Appointment to a leadership position may happen suddenly, as it did with me, but leadership development does not happen overnight. We, indeed, went through a transitional period in the Native American contextual movement. We began with no script, no examples, and no leaders. Those of us who were bold enough to break with older models of ministry practices chose to walk a new road that we believed was better. For better or for worse, William Bridges states,

> The new way of doing things represents a gamble: There is always the possibility it won't work. The very idea of doing something the new way may be crazy and it may be unrealistic to think that an individual or group can carry it off. They (or worst yet me) may even make a shameful mess of the effort.[2]

On previous occasions, I had battled with the fear of stepping into leadership moving into full-time ministry; but this time I chose to make the move, and now I live with the opportunity to create a new Wiconi.

Although I have fears of making these huge ministry changes, God has moved me down the road of contextual ministry, opening doors and creating opportunities. Fear over contextual ministry affects not only those involved in it, but also those on the margins and those non-contextual ministers who are weighing the pros and the cons before making a move to get on board. Lingenfelter observes, 'The question of risk lies at the root of our fears. Fear is always a significant obstacle to life of a Christian pilgrimage. Once we identify our fears, we may then deal with them through application of the truth of Scripture.'[3] Growth in my understanding of contextual ministry was a classic case of transition, where I truly felt the betwixt and between for years. I entered the transition world as a contextual leader, although I was unaware there were others across the country who also were doing

---

[2] Bridges, *Managing Transitions: Making the Most of Change*, p. 59.
[3] Lingenfelter, *Transforming Culture*, p. 61.

contextual ministry. In our region of the country, I took a group of people through the process of change and transition – including liminality – until we created an active contextual Native American ministry. In this process, Bridges notes, 'It was not the image of the land of milk and honey that got the people out of Egypt or through the wilderness to the promise land – it was Moses' skill as a transition leader'.[4] Our skills in leading people through transition happened at the grass roots local level, although we were not immediately accepted by everyone. Several major opinion leaders in the community required some convincing. I had to explain to them the concept of contextual ministry so that they would change how they viewed our ministry church plant. Everett Rogers explains the role of opinion leaders:

> *Opinion leadership* is the degree to which an individual is able to influence informally other individual's attitudes or overt behavior in a desired way with relative frequency. A *change agent* is an individual who attempts to influence client's innovation-decision in a direction that is deemed desirable by a change agency.[5]

Diffusion of Innovation in Native Ministries

Thus, innovative influence on a culture can bring about change either positively or negatively. In our movement, we are attempting to use a contextual approach that influences positive change as opposed to negative change. We desire to replace evangelism methods that have produced little or no results with methods that will make a positive impact. To accomplish this type of change (whether in our Native American culture or in any culture for that matter) requires the work of cultural insiders. Cultural insiders are needed because without an insider, 'there will not be genuine contextualization, but only surface level adaptations'.[6] The contextual movement works toward *innovation* not just an *adaptation* to the Native ministry world.

---

[4] Bridges, *Managing Transitions: Making the Most of Change*, pp. 37-38 (emphasis original).
[5] Rogers, *Diffusion of Innovations*, p. 38.
[6] Twiss, 'Rescuing Theology from the Cowboys', p. 113.

Stepping out to introduce innovation in a new context requires a very creative mind. Rogers writes, 'Diffusion is a special type of communication concerned with the spread of messages that are perceived as new ideas'.[7] I have been able to apply diffusion of innovation to the Native American contextualization movement and also to the recovery approach at the Brethren in Christ Overcomers treatment program. At the Brethren in Christ we have introduced new ideas and innovations of the contextual movement. With the treatment program, we have been able to introduce to the clients new ideas and ways of living so that they might change the image of life by which they have been living. During the transition time at the treatment center, the men in recovery discover such things as a better work ethic, positive relationship building, money management, child raising, and Christian biblical understanding. This new way of living is taught to the men throughout the three-month program, and it makes a difference in their lives, leading to a successful recovery from drugs and alcohol. They may have been aware of some of the new ideas, but they may have lacked the skills to apply them practically to their lives. The contextual model has enabled them to make those practical changes. Rogers further notes,

> Simply to regard the adaption of innovation as *rational* (defined as use of the most effective means to reach a given end) and to classify rejection as stupid is to fail to understand that individual innovation-decisions are idiosyncratic. They are based on an *individual's* perception of the innovation. Whether considered right or wrong by scientific experts who seek to evaluate an innovation objectively, adaptation or rejection is always 'right' in the eyes of the individual who made the innovation-decision (at least at the time of the decision is made).[8]

The majority of the clients at the Overcomers program are Native and mostly Navajo. The methods and approaches of treatment will result in the client's making a personal decision leading to recovery. The approach at the Overcomers is geared for this particular region and clientele. 'Since we seldom reflect on our

---

[7] Rogers, *Diffusion of Innovations*, p. 35.
[8] Rogers, *Diffusion of Innovations*, p. 116 (emphasis original).

underlying values, we assume everyone thinks like we do, and we imagine that anyone who reasons differently is incompetent, rude or not raised "properly".[9] The staff at the Brethren in Christ Overcomers have developed a program that see the men and their culture as normal and natural to them. This has made all the difference in their treatment.

Just as the Native American contextual ministry movement has met the need to develop ministry models created by Native Americans, the Brethren in Christ Overcomes treatment program was created by Native Americans to meet the needs for the alcohol recovery of Native Americans. Plueddemann further notes,

> It would be absurd to expect that a foreign 'expert' could teach a leadership course in Nigeria (or for that matter to Native Americans) without an understanding of the traditional cultural assumptions about how leaders are developed … in the Native American communities. [10]

I have come into leadership because I gained knowledge and understanding and trust from my Native community. The members of the community are the ones who bestow the role of leadership to a person, especially a person from within their own ranks. Lingenfelter shares a quote from Max DePree, that is appropriate here. DePree states, 'leadership is how one lives within a structure, respecting the people, accepting their differences, and engaging them in ways that inspire trust and transforms yet sustains relationships and structure'.[11]

The Native American urban world is similar to the church world in that Native People in the church are searching for direction. Their worlds are changing, with fewer and fewer people attending church. The urban Native world, away from the reservation, is a melting pot, where young people venture out and become absorbed into the urban life. Likewise, they are losing their Native identity, culture, language, and traditions with each passing year. (Similar to the way the church loses attendance). 'In this way, often inner-city Native people have struggled valiantly to maintain

---

[9] Plueddemann, *Leading Across Cultures*, p. 64.
[10] Plueddemann, *Leading Across Cultures*, p. 204.
[11] Lingenfelter, *Leading Cross-Culturally*, p. 99.

their cultural ways and identity in a world dominated by foreign ways'.[12] It is in and for this world that these contextual innovators are working.

Agents of Innovation and Change

Innovators and change agents live in the liminal stage most of the time, because they frequently move within a transitioning state, seeking for newness. 'I am convinced of this truth: The river of what God wants to do is flowing nearby every one of our ministries if we will just discover it'.[13] However, most traditional ministries are not aware that contextual ways of doing ministry even exist. Visioning, dreaming, being bold enough to change, and being creative is where the liminal stage does its best work. Seeing a glimpse of a preferred future, as Richard Twiss would say, is the key to bringing our Native American people closer to Jesus Christ. Creative thinking is one of a leader's 'primary responsibilities; for things to happen they have to dream and see the impossible ideas within their grasp'.[14]

Liminality and creativity go hand in hand. Transition and change happen as leaders buck the system and open the door for innovation to take root and grow. But there are too few of these creative leaders; their tribe must increase. Change and transition are difficult because they require thinking outside the box and coloring outside the lines. They require the daring to look around and envision what lies ahead, while asking, 'Is there a newer, more efficient method?'.[15]

William Bridges' Transitional Model might be summarized in these three stages: 1. Ending: people let go of old ways of doing things and who they were in the old situation. 2. Neutral Zone: People find themselves in a confusing, in-between state. They are no longer who they were and doing what they did in the past, and have not yet integrated a new identity. 3. New Beginning: People

---

[12] Twiss, 'Rescuing Theology from the Cowboys', p. 117.
[13] Southerland, *Transitioning: Leading Your Church Through Change*, p. 23.
[14] Chand and Murphey, *Futuring: Leading Your Church Into Tomorrow*, p. 123.
[15] Chand and Murphey, *Futuring: Leading Your Church Into Tomorrow*, p. 123.

start to take hold and grow familiar with the new identity and begin to identify with the (their) situation again.

My own journey is similar to that of Richard Twiss, who explains, 'As I look back on that time, I realize I was starting down the road of an internal, personal decolonization process and deconstruction of my conservative evangelical Christian philosophical introduction to biblical faith'.[16] My situation had me challenge my ideals and values concerning typical approaches to 'church'. I had been indoctrinated to a method of maintaining, when I so wanted to change the face of doing church so that Native American non-believers would have a culturally appropriate opportunity to meet Christ from within their cultural context. George Barna states the following with regard to evangelism, 'Much of evangelism fails to result in conversions. The task of the Christian, however, is to be faithful in sharing the gospel. It is the job of the Holy Spirit to complete the process by leading the non-believer to decide to follow Jesus Christ.'[17] I would argue, however, that the Christian also has the task of making the gospel understandable to the audience. Making the gospel more easily accessible for Native Americans by creating an approach different from the western model has been my calling from the start. The goal of this strategy is not to create more western-style churches but to adapt culturally. Barna states further, 'Success in evangelism is obedience to the call to evangelize, not the number of conversions in which a person plays a part'.[18] However, the appeal to 'obedience' can become an excuse for irrelevance and a justification for ineffective methods. My ultimate purpose is to know Christ and make him known, which means that I must create ways to present Jesus to Native People that remove any barriers to that task. It also means that leaders must help the group focus on their new identity in Christ and lead them in a process of commitment to Christ and to one another to be the people of God on mission together.[19]

---

[16] Twiss, 'Rescuing Theology from the Cowboys', p. 60.
[17] George Barna, *Evangelism That Works* (Ventura, CA: Regal Books, 1995), p. 72.
[18] Barna, *Evangelism That Works*, p. 72.
[19] Lingenfelter, *Leading Cross Culturally*, p. 80.

The process of change and transition through which I have passed to get where I am today was a journey of patience – patience with myself, patience with others around me, and patience with those opposed to my ministry direction. It was a long journey before the road smoothed out from a two track, to gravel, to pavement, to a highway. Looking back on how I felt at the beginning, as we created a contextual ministry, it was a feeling of being normal, natural, and indigenous. I felt like I had been gone for a long time and had finally come home. It was a journey of self-discovery, trying to find a way for my Potawatomi culture and tradition to fit with my faith in Jesus, a faith that had been so enmeshed with western culture that there was no room for me to move. I came down to what Lingenfelter calls the 'pilgrim principle'. He argues that contextualization should not isolate and detach the Native church from the universal church; but instead, the pilgrim principle 'draws the church in the direction of universals of the faith, rooted in obedience to Christ and the Scriptures'.[20] Contextualization should not be the adoption of anyone's imposed cultural traditions fabricated from their ancient pre-Christian past.

In taking this contextual position, I faced many obstacles that hindered my leadership development. There were such things as the following: loyalties to people who doubted my approach, fear of incompetence, uncertainty about taking the right path, fear of loss, not having the stomach for the hard part of the journey, and what I felt was my biggest personal failure, trusting God completely.[21] Fully trusting God as I entered ministry at the beginning meant that I was like a young child. I completely trusted, but as time went on and the waves began to get bigger and the wind began to blow the concerns of family life filled my mind. Bills had to be paid: school tuition, rent, car payment, groceries, and insurance all prevented me from jumping in fully. William Bridges uses a metaphor to describe management transition. He says that it is 'like learning to swim. Letting go of the edge and swimming. The teacher is saying "I won't let you sink." Without trust in the teacher, that step to independence and the mastery of a new skill

---

[20] Lingenfelter, *Transforming Culture*, p. 15.
[21] Heifetz, Linsky, and Grashow, *The Practice of Adaptive Leadership*, p. 247.

would have been less likely to happen. It is fear balanced against hope, it is trust that makes the difference.'[22] I had to trust the teacher – Jesus Christ. I say all this because it was truly about my ministry journey in the liminal time, a journey to become an effective leader. Sharing honestly, I want people to know me, to know that I am just a common man, pitiful in every way. Owning up to my short comings and my failures will make me the servant that God wants me to be.

Wiconi in Transition: Process of Liminality

These examples of change-transition and liminality offer a way of understanding the ministry's current experience of my position and the Wiconi organization.

> Liminality is a term that describes the transition process accompanying a change of state of social position. Therefore, liminality is a conscious awareness that as a group (or individual) one's status-role, and sequences-set in a society have been radically changed.[23]

Liminality aptly describes the current stage of Wiconi and my place in it. In many respects, what we are encountering parallels the rituals and ceremonies of my personal and community life as a Potawatomi Native. Victor Turner states, 'People at the center of ritual are liminal beings'.[24] This position is characterized by a sense of not fitting in totally in any one location. The loss of Richard Twiss, the transition and change of the Wiconi organization, and my leaving my secular employment all play a part in this ceremony. My situation plays out in people's lives in Native rituals throughout the world. Hiebert and Shaw note, 'They lose their status in normal society and enter a state of transition – a time during which they are in the cracks between two identities: neither here nor there, no longer the old but not yet the new'.[25] Yes, this is right where I am, but the reassuring thought is this: it is a normal

---

[22] Bridges, *Managing Transitions: Making the Most of Change*, p. 108.
[23] Roxburgh, *The Missionary Congregation, Leadership, and Liminality*, pp. 23-24.
[24] Turner, *The Ritual Process: Structure and Anti-Structure*, p. 96.
[25] Hiebert and Shaw, *Understanding Folk Religion*, p. 297.

position to be in. Changes have happened; they are happening new every day; and they will continue to happen in the lives of people. It is like shifting gears in a manual shift automobile. You have the metaphorical keys to start the vehicle of an idea, method, or approach to doing something. You put the keys in and start the process. You run it in first gear for a time until you get to a point to change direction, then you grab the shifter, depress the clutch, and move from first gear to neutral to second gear. Neutral is the position between changes, it is necessary in order to move to another gear. Most cultures or languages do not even have a name for it. The neutral zone is somewhere between was and what will be. The neutral zone occurs not only in organizations but also in individual's lives and in the history of whole societies.[26] Through our Christian history, societies have also gone through many major changes. The church we experience today had little in common with the first-century church, and syncretism has played a role in all of these changes. Syncretism has been a process throughout history. Syncretism and the liminal stage are part of the process of the neutral zone; it is for this reason that managing the neutral zone is so essential during a period of enormous change.[27] Managing these changes and transitions during the liminal or neutral zone is where my leadership style can play its biggest part. As an artist in pottery making, I understand the process of creating change. I take a lump of clay, and I handle it with controlled force. With gentle persuasion, I begin to shape the lump of clay and move it through several stages in order to produce an end product that emerges as a piece of art. Sharon Parks explains my example. She argues that we need

> a practice of leadership that is less like command and control and more like artistry. What they are practicing is both theory building, and case-in-point teaching is best understood as akin to processes of creativity-evoking innovation and a more adequate way of seeing ... in times of change.[28]

---

[26] Bridges, *Managing Transitions: Making the Most of Change*, p. 40.
[27] Bridges, *Managing Transitions: Making the Most of Change*, p. 42.
[28] Parks, *Leadership Can Be Taught*, p. 208.

For Native American people, there is no separation of secular and sacred. We are spiritual persons 100% of the time. Thus, unlike many western cultures, rituals and ceremonies are a natural part of life. 'Rituals take many diverse forms, yet all rituals have symbolic importance to the participants. There is a reason the ancients created the rite of passage. They knew the importance of rituals.'[29] I realize that what I am proposing is difficult for non-Native readers to understand, but it can increase their awareness of Native American beliefs and rituals of transition, change, and liminality as it relates to rites of passage. Twiss knew this well, and he states, 'By understanding the beliefs and attitudes of people from different backgrounds, we can build honest and open relationships. Native people need to be understood as a modern people who have a rich heritage and history in this country.'[30] I have always had to bend to the cultural ways of the west in order to navigate and survive within a different culture. By claiming the authenticity of my Native identity, I can begin to see my cultural understanding as a legitimate way of expressing myself without feeling that I am odd, wrong, or even backward. The familiar rituals of my world can show us all how to live more balanced lives. Roberta King shares how Native rituals and customs can be used as teaching that goes to the depth of hearts, giving 'counsel', 'advice', and speaking and showing the way we should walk.[31] Having to live in two worlds created a growing unrest in my soul about the dualistic gap that western Christianity had created in me.

Early white concepts of Native religion generally ranged from devil worship to mere paganism, from which Indians had to be won to Christ. By the turn of the 21st century, however, new respect for Native religion had arisen among white intellectuals, anthropologists in particular (and I would add theologians and missiologists).[32] There is a growing awareness of the usefulness of indigenous people's cultures for themselves. 'Culture also serves God's purposes. He uses it to shape the hearts of spiritual leaders.

---

[29] Lingenfelter, *Transforming Culture*, p. 166.
[30] Twiss, 'Rescuing Theology from the Cowboys', p. 68.
[31] King, *Pathways in Christian Music Communication*, p. 182.
[32] Jenkins, Philip, *Dream Catchers: How Mainstream America Discovered Native Spirituality* (New York: Oxford University Press, 2004), p. 83.

This means that culture can be appreciated and studied for its contributions as a heart-shaping drama in the leader's life story.'[33]

Creating Team in Liminality

The process of building and growing a team also involves rites of passage principles. There is the time of entering the process, and the liminal time in the relationship building. Once the team has been built, the group re-enters the ministry with a readiness to move forward. Creating a team begins with understanding the process in. Robbins and Finley note the following: 'In developing strong teams, understanding and valuing differences is essential. But in adapting to change, understanding and valuing commonalities is the key. We grow by focusing on how we are unique, we progress by focusing on how we are similar.'[34] Team-building requires patience and sensitivity, especially in organizational change and transition. 'All people know is that things "Feel different" around the organization. As with the coming of a new season the weather of everyday activities may slip back and forth for a while, and you may be unsure whether the new season is really at hand.'[35] With Wiconi, we have a history of ups and downs but mostly ups. But there is a sense that trust has not fully taken hold, and moving forward boldly has not yet become our priority. I believe God is saying, 'Go for it! Be strong. Dream new dreams, Honor the past, but do not live there. God has too much in store for us in the promise lands he has prepared for our churches.'[36] But it's up to us to decide to go forward – the past was full of great moments, and those times are a shadow of the low periods. I was a part of many of those positive ministry times; therefore, while in the liminal stage of team building, I know never to denigrate the past. 'Many managers in their enthusiasm for a future that is going to be better than the past, ridicule or talk slightingly of the old ways of doing

---

[33] McNeal, *A Work of Heart*, p. 73.
[34] Harvey Robbins and Michael Finley, *Why Change Doesn't Work: Why Initiatives Go Wrong and How to Try Again – And Succeed* (Albany, NY: Petersons, 1997), p. 56.
[35] Bridges, *Managing Transitions: Making the Most of Change*, p. 92.
[36] Nelson and Appel, *How to Change Your Church (Without Killing It)*, p. xvii.

things. In doing so they consolidate the resistance against the transition.'[37]

My movement through the change and transition stage of liminality reminds me of a story I once heard about a new pastor at a church. He wanted to make changes too fast. He wanted to move the piano to the other side of the platform, so on the next Sunday, the congregation found the piano moved. That pastor was fired. Another pastor was called, and he wanted to make the same change. Sometime later, the first pastor returned to the church to visit; and, to his surprise, the piano was on the opposite side of the church platform. He asked the new pastor how he had gotten the people to accept the change. He said, 'Every week I moved the piano about an inch toward the other side of the church platform.' Making changes will take time. William Bridges says, 'You would do well to set short range goals for people to aim toward and to establish check points along the way toward long-term outcomes that you are seeking'.[38]

Another example of how to implement change comes from Pastor Bill Hybels, who learned it from his former Bible college instructor, Professor Beleziken. He advised that to create needed change, the leader must, from time-to-time, stretch the limits to force change. He called it three steps forward and two steps back.[39] He would have argued that pushing the piano all the way was too much but taking inch at a time was too little. When making change and transitions, one way is to push the limits in the liminal stage in order to produce some forward motion. By pushing beyond the comfort zone and then moving backward a bit, you can break a barrier that allows for change above the initial starting point. 'If you don't occasionally exceed your formal authority you are not pushing the envelope.'[40]

Clients in the Overcomers program are taken through many changes that push them beyond their comfort zones. During the liminal period, they are taken further than they have gone before, and this makes moving toward recovery more acceptable. The

---

[37] Bridges, *Managing Transitions: Making the Most of Change*, p. 34.
[38] Bridges, *Managing Transitions: Making the Most of Change*, p. 46.
[39] Nelson and Appel, *How to Change Your Church (Without Killing It)*, p. 281.
[40] Heifetz, Linsky, and Grashow, *The Practice of Adaptive Leadership*, p. 23.

same is true with people in an organization and for those in leadership. It is important for leaders to remember the people who are going through change, keeping in mind that their pain is real. Part of the leader's role is to make changes bearable. The pace of change is critical: 'It's fine to get started with change right away, but from the start you need to think of this as a long, complex process you are tracking. Transition is going to take months, at least.'[41] Whether in recovery from addiction or going through organization or leadership changes, William Bridges advises us to, 'Be careful that in urging people to turn away from the past you don't drive them away from you or from the new direction that the organization (or behavior) needs to take'.[42]

Leadership for the Liminal Phase of Change

When we go through rites of passage, it creates discomfort, and we look for answers to help us face the issues. 'When everything is going smoothly it's often hard to change things. Outsiders to an organization (or issue) who do not know much about the subject are often the ones who come up with the breakthrough answer.'[43] This is what Richard Twiss and others are able to see and do within their context. These creative people play a significant role in rites of passage; they are able to see what needs to take place, and they have a God-given boldness and perseverance. They are people, 'called of God', as leaders for the liminal phase of change. Twiss, one of these liminal leaders, says,

> In light of significant opposition, criticism and rejection the men and women identified as innovators in my research have, and continue to 'love prophetically' calling others to join together in making Jesus known and living out that faith in partnership with what Creator is doing.[44]

These liminal leaders, like a shaman or some other special leader in our Native traditional world, walk in the two worlds of

---

41 Bridges, *Managing Transitions: Making the Most of Change*, p. 91.
42 Bridges, *Managing Transitions: Making the Most of Change*, p. 35.
43 Bridges, *Managing Transitions: Making the Most of Change*, p. 42.
44 Twiss, 'Rescuing Theology from the Cowboys', p. 121.

Native tradition and Christian faith. When transition and change happen in our world, we often question whether the whole thing is worth it, and we grow anxious and frustrated. When change interrupts the balance of our life, we call on these liminal leaders as sent by the Creator. The operating assumption has been that spiritual leaders already understand spiritual formation, and they are materially applying these disciplines into their own lives. It is a discipline not taught from books, but learned from experience in and from contextual ministry.

Pacing change is very important. When you are leading change, you must have a vision to lead people through the in-between zone. You must take the time to plant vision with key leaders before sharing vision with everyone, making the process to the preferred future a deliberate one. Heifetz describes the work of leading through transition as 'adaptive work', which requires a learning strategy. A leader has to engage people in facing challenge, adjusting their values, changing perspectives, and developing new habits of behaviors. All of these and other modification to an individual or group are needed for a successful transition to take place.

Death as a Liminal Crisis and Opportunity for Transition and Change

Richard Twiss' death created a crisis in Wiconi, and the local leaders and followers resorted to traditions. Many of them returned to patterns established in our tribes to deal with and help the transition of the loved one's passing. Our traditions call for a year-long time of mourning that involves not saying the person's name and cutting our hair, along with several other rituals. These times are marked as a time of transition, which gives us space to cope with the immense changes. 'We call this time the "neutral zone": it's when the critical psychological realignments and re-patterning take place.'[45] As painful as it is, the neutral zone is the best chance to be creative, to develop into what we need to become, and to

---

[45] Bridges, *Managing Transitions: Making the Most of Change*, p. 5.

renew ourselves. It is a time when innovation is most possible and when the organization can most easily be revitalized.[46]

After Richard's death, Wiconi entered an 'in-between time' in which 'We are not what we used to be and we are still becoming what we are not yet. In this in-between time, we experience confusion, deep loss, fear, the unknown searching, and despair.'[47] Richard was well aware of transition and change, having spent the last 20 years creating and leading Wiconi. Richard had points in his life that led to major changes. Some he considered symbolic and benchmarks that led to his developing Wiconi.

Many years ago, while Richard was pastoring an all-white congregation, the Lord gave him the vision to create a ministry that would minister to Natives in a manner far different from any that had been done before. This was the beginning of Wiconi. This major change would take Richard on a journey that would affect the lives of many other Native leaders to whom the Lord had given the same vision for ministry. His ministry would enter a ten-year time of influencing a generation of Native and non-Native ministry leaders with the start of the Many Nations One Voice conferences held across the country. It was toward the end of these conferences that the move was made to create a Family Camp. Every move of the Wiconi life, from one stage to the next, was entered with discernment, confirmation, and prayer.

Near the end of his life, Richard called together a core group of colleagues to spend a weekend in conversation about what Wiconi should do for the future. In that meeting, Richard made the decision to work more in his home community and to travel less than before. This was a hard decision, because it was the traveling that paid the bills. Richard changed his mode of operation and began to become more a part of his community. This was one of the last major changes he was willing to make just a couple of years before his passing.

Each of these changes and transitions in the life of Richard and the Wiconi organization is an example of a rite of passage. In the Native world, all of life is sacred; and each change in status,

[46] Bridges, *Managing Transitions: Making the Most of Change*, p. 9.
[47] Twiss, 'Rescuing Theology from the Cowboys', p. 35.

life situation, and organizational move, is seen as a ceremony. Ritual and ceremony enable us to start a new phase of life, to learn to adjust and manage life in the new situation, and then to step forward as a new creation, in new status, or as a new organization.

Liminality offers a rich resource of experimental maps that can suggest ways ahead for Wiconi in framing a response to their changed ministry situation.[48] This betwixt-and-between period in our Native traditions has purpose; it is at the core of our ritual and ceremony. Many Native traditions have found ways to look at the time of transition with optimism. When decisions need to be made, we look to the Creator for answers and guidance; when we have lost our direction, we seek a vision; when children grow, we have rites of passage called puberty rites. 'This liminal place provides initiates with a chaotic limbo condition of transition "betwixt and between" the clearly defined statuses and roles of childhood and adulthood in their society.'[49] People and children need these transitional times. Some are expected, and we prepare for them with rituals; but in the case of death, we seek wisdom from our elders who have experienced death over the years.

The death of Richard Twiss was a tragic loss for Wiconi, and it created a leadership vacuum in the contextual movement. However, we may discover in retrospect that the transition of his death turns out to be Richard's gift to us all in disguise. What if this very distressing loss is a symbolic event? Richard was well aware of his mortality, and he was making plans for Wiconi's long-term continuation. Although he was a brilliant man, he did not know the day of his departure. Therefore, he focused on building a competent leadership team for the future.

We all know how a person feels at a time of such loss, and yet the ending must be dealt before we can move on to whatever comes next in our lives. The new growth cannot take root in ground that is still covered with old habits, attitudes, and outlooks; and endings are the clearing process.[50] Someone at the memorial

---

[48] Roxburgh, *The Missionary Congregation, Leadership, and Liminality*, p. 23.

[49] A.H. Mathias Zahniser, *Symbol and Ceremony: Making Disciples Across Cultures: Innovations in Mission* (Federal Way, WA: MARC Publications, 1997), pp. 92-93.

[50] Bridges, *Managing Transitions: Making Sense of Life's Changes*, p. 108.

for Richard said it very well: 'Very truly I tell you, unless a kernel of wheat falls to the ground and dies, it remains only a single seed. But if it dies, it produces many seeds' (Jn 12.24 NIV). This multiplication of seeds is now taking place with the various ministries and people involved with Wiconi International. These ministries realize that they must now step up and fill the gap that Richard had filled with his larger-than-life persona. People know what needs to happen, but they are looking to someone else to lead the way. With my new position, I feel I am helping these minsters realize that a new era is taking place, and it will now be up to us to carry on contextual ministry with Richard's vision as our guide. Wouldn't it be something if Wiconi – with its rich past, committed people, and strategic resources – could be re-ignited for a new era of ministry during this time of change?

Appendix A

Questionnaire for BICO Clients

The following questions are part of a research project being conducted by Casey Church. Casey is a doctoral student and the Native man who conducted the sweat lodge and other cultural activities for the BIC Overcomers program.

Casey is requesting your participation in the following questionnaire. We at the BIC highly recommend this research project. It will benefit our overall programing by giving us valuable information to evaluate our program.

By completing and returning this questionnaire you are giving permission for the BIC and Casey to use the information for evaluation and his research. The responses you give to the questions will be used only by the BIC and Casey's research project. You may view the results of the questionnaire and also the completed research paper upon request. Your responses will remain anonymous unless you indicate otherwise.

There are two parts to this questionnaire. The first is a section of Yes or No questions.

Your Name: _____

1. The Bible lessons at the BIC Overcomers were helpful to my over-all recovery? Yes No
2. I believe the BIC's Overcomers program has helped me to recover from my alcohol problem? Yes No
3. I believe the BIC Overcomers program has helped my spiritual life as a believer in Jesus. Yes No
4. The Native sweat lodge ceremony had a positive effect on my self-identity. Yes No
5. The sweat lodge ceremony had a positive effect on my recovery? Yes No
6. Learning the songs with the drum and singing was a positive experience. Yes No

7. I believe the use of Native rituals at the BIC Overcomers had a positive effect on my spiritual life as a Native person. Yes No
8. The faith based program along with the Native rituals had a positive effect on my recovery. Yes No
9. I grew in my faith and spiritual life as a follower of the Jesus way as result of the BIC Overcomers program. Yes No
10. My experience at the BIC Overcomers was a positive experience. Yes No
11. Do you feel the concept of Hozho (beauty, balance, and harmony) were present within the program. Yes No
12. I give my permission to use my name in the research project by Casey Church. Yes No

Questions for the Overcomers Clients

Part II

This section is an opportunity for you to express yourself in short answers about the BIC Overcomer's treatment program. Your responses will be a way for the BIC and Casey's project to hear in your own words about your experience while at the BIC Overcomers program.

In a couple of sentences or paragraphs answer the following questions:

1. I give permission for the BIC and Casey Church to use my responses for the benefit of the Program. Yes No
2. Are you familiar with the Navajo concept of Hozho (beauty, balance, and harmony)? Did you feel Hozho while at the Overcomers Program? Explain
3. What are the most important things you have learned while attending the Overcomers program?
4. How was the use of Native American rituals helpful to your spiritual growth while at the program?
5. What did you think of the use of Native prayer, rituals, and music in this program?
6. Do you feel/think the program would be as effective without the use of Native America traditional ways? Explain you answer.
7. What is it about the program you feel has helped you the most?

8. What do you see is the benefit of learning Christian songs sung using the drum?

Appendix B

Questionnaire for BIC Staff, Denominational Leaders, and Home Living Coordinators

The following questions are part of a research project being conducted by Casey Church. Casey is a doctoral student and the Native man who conducted the sweat lodge and other cultural activities for the BIC Overcomers program.

Casey is requesting your participation in the following questionnaire. We at the BIC highly recommend this research project. It will benefit our overall programing by giving us valuable information to evaluate our program.

By completing and returning this questionnaire you are giving permission for the BIC and Casey to use the information for evaluation and research. The responses you give to the questions will only be used by the BIC and Casey's research project. You may view the results of the questionnaire upon request. You can further have access to the completed research paper also upon request. Your responses will remain anonymous unless you indicate otherwise.

Some of the questions may sound redundant but please try to answer as completely as you can. Further, your answers may be used in telling the story of the BIC Overcomers residential treatment program and your responses can become a significance portion of its content.

Note: your responses do not all have to be positive, if there is any question of a negative nature please feel free to include it in your answer.

Part I

1. Your Name:
2. Your Title:
3. I give permission for the BIC and Casey Church to use my responses for the benefit of the Program. Yes No
4. I give permission for the BIC and Casey Church to use my name in the telling of the Overcomers treatment programs story. Yes No
5. Can you describe your role – How are you involved with the Overcomers?
6. Are you familiar with the Navajo concept of Hozho (beauty, balance and harmony)? Explain.
7. What do you believe are the characteristics that make the Overcomers program successful?
8. What dreams, goals for the program's future do you have?
9. What are the most important things you have learned while working with the BIC and the Overcomers program?
10. What are your thoughts on the Native American prayer practices used in the Overcomers treatment program?
11. How do you see the Native America ritual and practice in this Christian residential treatment program benefiting the client's spiritual development?
12. What are your thoughts on the use of Christian songs sung on the drum and its effect on the client's spiritual formation and subsequent recovery?
13. Can you tell me of a situation you have seen where these prayer practices and rituals were played out with positive or negative results?
14. If you had the option, would you personally continue to use these methods?
15. What is the most useful aspect in your perspective of the use of Native American practices in the program? (prayer, rituals, and music)
16. Do you feel/think the program would be as effective without the use of Native America traditional ways? Explain your answer.

17. What is it about the program, in your perspective, that seems to be the key to its success in the Native men's recovery?
18. What are your thoughts on the use of the sweat lodge where Christian songs and prayers are said in the conjunction with the treatment program?
19. What do you think needs to be emphasized more in the program? Can you explain why it is important?
20. What is the most important lesson you have learned from your involvement in the Overcomers program?
21. What do you think are the greatest strengths of the program?
22. What are the priorities of the program as you see them?
23. In one sentence what do you feel makes the program work so well?
24. What do you think are the weaknesses of the program? If you note a weakness please suggest how it can be improved?

Part II

Table Display illustration with typical Christian and Native American artifacts

A table display is placed in front of you with Christian and Native cultural items on the table. The items are: the Bible, an Eagle feather on top of the Bible, a communion set, an abalone shell with sage, a hand drum, a Christian hymnal, a Native flute, a crucifix, and a Native prayer pipe.

- What is your response to the table display?

- What is your response to the following Vignette?
  A Native man named Lester Falls Apart has an alcohol problem and has just self-admitted himself into the Overcomers treatment program this morning. He has heard many interesting things about the program. He asked you about the program's incorporation of both Native American prayer practices and rituals with

Christian prayer ways in this Christ-centered program. What would you tell him to help him understand what the program is all about?

APPENDIX C

QUESTIONNAIRE FOR WICONI FAMILY CAMP ATTENDERS

The following questions are part of a research project being conducted by Casey Church. Casey is a doctoral student and the Native man who is now the director of Wiconi International and also director of the Family Camp and further conducts the sweat lodge and other cultural activities at the Wiconi Family Camp.

Casey is requesting your participation in the following questionnaire. By completing and returning this questionnaire you are giving permission for Casey Church Wiconi International to use your responses. You can further have access to the completed research paper upon request. Some of the questions may sound redundant but please try to answer as complete as you can. Further your answers may be used in telling the story of the Wiconi Family Camp in subsequent writings and your responses can become a significance portion of its content.

Note: your responses do not all have to be positive, if there is any question of a negative nature please feel free to include it in your answer.

This section is an opportunity for you to express yourself in short answers about Wiconi International and the Wiconi Family Camp. In a couple of sentences or paragraphs answer the following questions:

1. I give permission for Casey Church to use my responses for his doctoral studies and for the benefit of Wiconi International. Yes No
2. What is your name? What is your ethnic background or tribal heritage?
3. Are you familiar with contextual ministry approaches that the Wiconi Family Camp incorporates? Yes No

4. What are the most important things you have learned while attending the Wiconi Family Camp?

5. How was the use of Native American rituals helpful to your spiritual growth while at the Family Camp?

6. What did you think of the contextual use of Native prayer, rituals, and music while at the camp?

7. Do you feel/think the program would be as effective without the use of Native America traditional ways? Explain your answer.

8. What one aspect about the Wiconi Family Camp do you feel has helped you the most?

9. What do you see is the benefit of learning Christian songs sung using the drum and other contextual songs sung by the contextual musicians?

10. What do you believe are the characteristics that make the Wiconi Family Camp successful?

11. What greater dreams, goals for the camp's future do you have?

12. What are the most important things you have learned while attending and participating in the Wiconi Family Camp?

13. What are your thoughts on the Native American prayer rituals and ceremonies used at the Wiconi Family Camp?

14. How has the use of Native America ritual and practice at the camp benefited the spiritual development of you and other campers?

15. What are your thoughts on the use of Christian songs sung on the drum and its effect on yours and other's spiritual formation and faith journey?

16. Can you tell of a situation where these prayer practices and rituals were played out with positive or negative results?

17. If you had the option, would you personally continue to use these methods learned at the camp?

18. What is the most useful aspect, in your perspective, of the use of Native American practices in the program?

19. Do you feel/think the program would be as effective without the use of Native America traditional ways? Explain your answer.

20. What is it about the Family Camp, in your perspective, that seems to be the key to its success?

21. What are your thoughts on the use of the sweat lodge where Christian songs and prayers are said in conjunction with your personal Christian faith?

22. What do you think needs to be emphasized more at the camp? Can you explain?

23. What is the most important lesson you have learned from your involvement with Wiconi International and its ministry approach?

24. What do you think are the greatest strengths of Wiconi International?

25. What are the priorities of Wiconi International as you see them?

26. In one sentence what do you feel makes Wiconi International and the Family Camp worth continuing?

27. What do you think are the weaknesses of Wiconi International and the Family Camp? If you note a weakness please suggest how it can be improved?

APPENDIX D

WICONI'S MISSION AND VALUES

Envisioning possibilities and creating opportunities for the betterment of our Native People and communities for generations to come.

Mission

- The mission of Wiconi International is to work for the well-being of our Native people by advancing cultural formation, indigenous education, spiritual awareness, and social justice connected to the teachings and life of Jesus, through an indigenous worldview framework.
- Wiconi International is a Native founded and led, not-for-profit organization that is community-based, beginning in the Portland/Vancouver Metro area. Our mission can best be illustrated with a four-quadrant circle representing four major forces or sets of factors that together must come into balance if a preferred future is to be realized; these are, Family, Community, Education, and Spirituality. The ways these forces in our circle are expressed organizationally are woven throughout our Guiding Values.

Guiding Values

- We seek to operate within a historical indigenous worldview, with contemporary applications, which is rooted in tribal cultures and the recognition that all life comes from, and is sustained by, a loving Creator, whom we embrace in Jesus the Christ. Our approach to serving our Native communities is informed and inspired by Lakota Traditional Values and the Seven Directions tradition of North, East, South, West, Up, Down, and Inward. It is spiritual, intuitive, deeply relational, fluid, and always community-based, seeking the common good.
- **North (Wisdom):** Wisdom is the ability to make good decisions, not just for personal success, but for family and community benefit too. Wisdom leads to the center of community well-being, which is the promotion, and support of family, cultural and spiritual values.

Education: Indigenous education is a key to creating a better future for our Native communities. We are deeply committed to creating better ways to do education rooted in a Native worldview, cultural understandings, and spiritual reality. We host an annual cross-cultural learning experience on the Rosebud Lakota/Sioux Reservation, participate in the North American Institute of Indigenous Theological Studies.

- **East (Fortitude):** Fortitude can be seen as the inner strength or inner fire that allows an individual to persevere in the face of adversity. Family: In the face of hostile political policies, centuries of colonialism, and socio-economic disparities, we choose to stand in the strength and grace of a good gospel as a voice for justice, reconciliation, and peace. To create a preferred future, in part, we host our annual *Mini Wiconi Wacipi* 'Living Waters Powwow' and Family Camp, promoting Native cultural and spiritual values while inviting community participation.

- **South (Generosity):** Generosity is giving of possessions, time, and energy to others so that they may be helped, encouraged, and blessed. Community: Each year, seeking the common good of the city, we help organize and serve, with a staff of dozens of volunteers, several other Native organizations cultural events, including Powwows, festivals and reconciliation gatherings to demonstrate peace and generosity.

- **West (Courage):** Courage is the willingness to put oneself in harm's way to protect family and community or to advance a higher cause or purpose. Courage is a necessary quality for community and spiritual leaders to make the needed sacrifices for good leadership. Education & Community: We seek to work for and stand for what is right, even when it is unpopular. Practically, young leaders participating in our Salmon Nation Internship Program, an inter-faith, multi-cultural, year-long leadership development experience, will learn to become better human beings by increasing their capacity to love deeply, serve generously, care sacrificially, walk respectfully, and embrace others. It takes courage to want to be this kind of person.

- **Up (Honor):** Honor is having integrity and honest character – being one who can be trusted. All human beings, and leaders in particular, therefore, must find help from above. Spirituality & Community: We provide spiritual and relational encouragement for our national tribal and Native organizational leaders by hosting the annual national tribal leaders prayer breakfast for the National Congress of American Indians.

- **Down (Respect):** Respect is understanding and embracing the sacredness and value of all creation, including people, animals, and earth. It informs the decisions we make every day about how to live in harmonious relationship with all living things. Family & Community: We are spiritual beings who learn to live in a loving, respectful, and generous way with our family, neighbors, and community. One way we do this is by creating volunteer opportunities between non-Native and Native people that are focused on practical assistance and relationship building that helps to eliminate ignorance and prejudice, leading to friendship and mutual awareness, in the midst of beautiful diversity.

- **Inward (Humility):** Humility is the core value – it is understood that only Creator is sacred or perfect and human beings at their very best, by comparison, are pitiful. There is a fundamental understanding that our very existence is a gift from our Creator and accordingly we live with humility toward and for the well-being of all things. Spirituality: All human beings desire a meaningful, enriching, fulfilling, and good life with their family, friends, and community. The ability to do this, however, is difficult. We embrace Jesus the Christ as this way, this truth, and this life to empower us to live in a sacred and humble way.

GLOSSARY

cedar:
Cedar is one of the most important sacred herbs used by the Lakota and other Native Americans for ceremony. The importance and reason for its use by the Native Americans has been echoed by several unrelated cultures throughout the world. Cedar is for the aid of visions and for helping the body and mind in times of great spiritual anxiety and stress.[1]

contextualization:
'In recent days missiologists have settled on the term contextualization to describe this task of understanding, communicating and expressing our faith in culturally relevant ways.'[2]

incense:
'Incense is defined as a material that is burned to produce an odor, usually fragrant, and is also referred to as the perfume or fumigation itself that is produced from the burning of plant and other materials.'[3]

Native American:
A member of any of the aboriginal peoples of the western hemisphere; especially: a Native American of North America and especially the United States.[4]

Native American contextual ministry:
Native American contextual ministry is the authentic use of Native American cultural forms of worship and prayer, practiced as

---

[1] Hughes, *The Incense Bible*, p. 138.
[2] Douglas Hayward, 'The Foundation for Critical Contextualization: Preliminary Considerations for Doing Contextualization Among First Nations Christians', *Journal of North American Institute for Indigenous Theological Studies* 6 (2008), p. 144.
[3] Kerry Hughes, *The Incense Bible: Plant Scents That Transcend World Culture, Medicine, and Spirituality* (Philadelphia, PA: Haworth Press, 2007), p. 8.
[4] *Merriam-Webster's Dictionary of English Usage* (Springfield, MA: Merriam-Webster, Inc., 1994).

Christian expressions. Whereas non-contextual ministry use only western methods of worship and prayer.

Pipe Ceremony:
The pipe is one of the central ceremonial objects of many American Indian groups. It was considered a microcosm, its parts and its decorative colors and motifs corresponding to the essential parts of the universe. It was smoked in personal prayer as well as at collective rites. Because of the narcotic effect of the tobacco and the symbolism of the indrawn and ascending smoke, the calumet was employed as a means of communication between the spirit world and humans.[5]

sage:
'Sage is one of the most important sacred herbs used by Lakota and other Native Americans for ceremonies and rituals.'[6]

smudging:
The use of smudging can be described many ways in several different tribal cultures. Corky Alexander writes the following after interviewing several Native leaders on the topic:

> The smudge is a cleansing or purification ceremony that cleanses body, soul, and spirit. It is done by lighting sage, sweet grass, or cedar, and then blowing out the fire causing it to smoke in a shell. In order to obtain cleansing, the Native person pulls the smoke onto themselves while the one burning the sage waves an eagle feather or fan to move the smoke.[7]

spiritual formation:
According to Dallas Willard, spiritual formation is the 'transformation of professing Christians into Christlikeness.'[8]

---

[5] *Merriam-Webster's Dictionary of English Usage.*
[6] Hughes, *The Incense Bible*, p. 8.
[7] Corky Alexander, *Native American Pentecost: Praxis, Contextualization, Transformation* (Cleveland, TN: Cherohala Press, 2012), p. 54.
[8] Willard, Dallas, 'Spiritual Formation as a Natural Part of Salvation', in Jeffrey P. Greenman and George Kalantzis (eds.), *Life in the Spirit: Spiritual Formation in Theological Perspective* (Downers Grove, IL: Inter-Varsity Press, 2010), p. 45.

sweat lodge:
A sweat lodge is a hut or lodge used for ritual purification. Its use originated with Native Americans – for whom it remains a significant ceremony – but it is now common among other non-Indian groups who recognize its health as well as spiritual benefits. The structure of the sweat lodge is usually made of bent saplings and skin or blanket coverings, and it is heated by steam from water poured on hot stones. A ceremony typically surrounds the lodge's construction and use. Some groups believe the lodge becomes a symbolic center in which the six cardinal directions, the past and present, and the human and spiritual worlds are connected.[9]

sweet grass:
Sweet grass is used by a number of Native American tribes for various purposes, including as a medicine by the Plains Indians and as a fiber for such things as in baskets or mats by the Northeastern tribes. Many of these tribes also use sweet grass ceremonially, for purification, for the sweet smell, for smoking, for protection. It can also be used as an insecticide and as a hair wash.[10]

syncretism:
Terry LeBlanc states, 'syncretism simply means taking non-biblical Native beliefs and practices and mixing them into Christian beliefs and practices so that the resultant system has borrowed from each of the contributing systems but is purely neither'.[11]

tobacco:
Tobacco is used as an incense by many (but not all) tribes in the United States. Native American author Basil Johnston describes the use of tobacco in the following terms: 'Tobacco is burned as an offering, as a way to give thanks, as a way of recognizing and honoring the Great Mystery'.[12]

---

[9] *Merriam-Webster's Dictionary of English Usage.*
[10] Hughes, *The Incense Bible*, p. 136.
[11] Terry LeBlanc, 'Culture, Faith and Mission: Creating the Future', *The Journal of the North American Institute for Indigenous Theological Studies* 1 (2003), p. 153.
[12] Basil Johnston, *Ojibway Heritage* (Toronto, Ontario: McClelland & Stewart, 2011), p. 43.

traditional Native American prayer rituals:
Traditional Native American prayer rituals are the prayer practices conducted by Native American people before they were influenced by or rejected for western forms of prayer.

BIBLIOGRAPHY

Alexander, Corky, *Native American Pentecost: Praxis, Contextualization, Transformation* (Cleveland, TN: Cherohala Press, 2012).

American Heritage College Dictionary (Boston, MA: Houghton Mifflin, 1985).

Barna, George, *Evangelism That Works* (Ventura, CA: Regal Books, 1995).

Bridges, William, *Managing Transitions: Making Sense of Life's Changes* (Boston, MA: Da Capo Press, 2004).

—*Managing Transitions: Making the Most of Change* (Boston, MA: Da Capo Press, 2009).

Chand, Samuel R., and Cecil B. Murphey, *Futuring: Leading Your Church Into Tomorrow* (Grand Rapids, MI: Baker Books, 2002).

Charisma House Staff and Passio Faith, *The Spiritual Warfare Bible: Modern English Version* (Lake Mary, FL: Charisma House, 2014).

Gilliland, Dean S., *Pauline Theology and Mission Practice* (Eugene, OR: Wipf and Stock Publishers, 1996).

Greenman, Jeffrey, and George Kalantzis, *Life in the Spirit: Spiritual Formation in Theological Perspective* (Downers Grove, IL: Inter-Varsity Press, 2010).

Hayward, Douglas, 'The Foundation for Critical Contextualization: Preliminary Considerations for Doing Contextualization Among First Nations Christians', *Journal of North American Institute for Indigenous Theological Studies* 6 (2008), pp. 59-77.

Heifetz, Ronald A., and Marty Linsky, *Leadership on the Line: Staying Alive Through the Dangers of Leading* (Cambridge, MA: Harvard Business Review Press, 2013).

Heifetz, Ronald A., Marty Linsky, and Alexander Grashow, *The Practice of Adaptive Leadership: Tools and Tactics for Changing Your Organization and the World* (Cambridge, MA: Harvard Business Review Press, 2013).

Hiebert, Paul G., and R. Daniel Shaw, *Understanding Folk Religion* (Grand Rapids, MI: Baker Academic, 2000).

Hiebert, Paul G., *Anthropological Insights for Missionaries* (Grand Rapids, MI: Baker Academic, 1986).

Hughes, Kerry, *The Incense Bible: Plant Scents That Transcend World Culture, Medicine, and Spirituality* (Philadelphia, PA: Haworth Press, 2007).

Hybels, Bill, *Courageous Leadership: Field-Tested Strategy for the 360° Leader* (Grand Rapids, MI: Zondervan, 2012).

Jenkins, Philip, *Dream Catchers: How Mainstream America Discovered Native Spirituality* (New York: Oxford University Press, 2004).

Johnston, Basil, *Ojibway Heritage* (Toronto, Ontario: McClelland & Stewart, 2011).

King, Roberta R., *Pathways in Christian Music Communication: The Case of the Senufo of Cote D'Ivoire* (Eugene, OR: Pickwick Publications, 2009).

Kraft, Charles H., *Appropriate Christianity* (Pasadena, CA: William Carey Library, 2005).

LeBlanc, Terry, 'Culture, Faith and Mission: Creating the Future', *The Journal of the North American Institute for Indigenous Theological Studies* 1 (2003), pp. 149-77.

Lingenfelter, Sherwood G., *Agents of Transformation: A Guide for Effective Cross-Cultural Ministry* (Grand Rapids, MI: Baker Academic, 1996).

—*Leading Cross-Culturally: Covenant Relationships for Effective Christian Leadership* (Grand Rapids, MI: Baker Academic, 2008).

—*Transforming Culture: A Challenge for Christian Mission* (Grand Rapids, MI: Baker Academic, 1998).

Mahdi, Louise C., Steven Foster, and Meredith Little, *Betwixt & Between: Patterns of Masculine and Feminine Initiation* (Peru, IL: Open Court, 1987).

Mayhall, C. Wayne, 'Effective Evangelism: To Know Christ and to Make Him Known', *Christian Research Institute* 31.4 (2008), Online Journal, http://www.equip.org.

McNeal, Reggie, *A Work of Heart: Understanding How God Shapes Spiritual Leaders* (San Francisco, CA: Jossey Bass, 2011).

Medicine, Beatrice, and Sue-Ellen Jacobs, *Learning to Be an Anthropologist and Remaining Native: Selected Writings* (Champaign, IL: University of Illinois Press, 2001).

Neill, Stephen, and Owen Chadwick, *A History of Christian Missions* (New York: Penguin Books, 1990).

Nelson, Alan, and Gene Appel, *How to Change Your Church (Without Killing It)* (Nashville, TN: Word Publishing, 2000).

Parks, Sharon D., *Leadership Can Be Taught: A Bold Approach for a Complex World* (Cambridge, MA: Harvard Business Review Press, 2013).

Plueddemann, James E., *Leading Across Cultures: Effective Ministry and Mission in the Global Church* (Downers Grove, IL: InterVarsity Press, 2009).

Pratt, Richard H., 'The Official Report of the Nineteenth Annual Conference of Charities and Correction, 1892', in *Americanizing the American Indians: Writings by the 'Friends of the Indian'* (Cambridge, MA: Harvard University Press, 1973), pp. 46-59.

Quinn, Robert E., *Deep Change: Discovering the Leader Within* (San Francisco: Jossey-Bass, 1996).

Richardson, Rick, *Evangelism Outside the Box: New Ways to Help People Experience the Good News* (Downers Grove, IL: Inter-Varsity Press, 2009).

Robbins, Harvey, and Michael Finley, *Why Change Doesn't Work: Why Initiatives Go Wrong and How to Try Again – And Succeed* (Albany, NY: Petersons, 1997).

Rogers, Everett, *Diffusion of Innovations* (New York: Free Press, 2010).

Roxburgh, Alan J., *The Missionary Congregation, Leadership, and Liminality* (New York: Bloomsbury Academic, 1997).

Smith, C.S., and Bill McCartney, *Whiteman's Gospel* (Winnipeg, Manitoba: Intertribal Christian Communications, 1998).

Southerland, Dan, *Transitioning: Leading Your Church Through Change* (Grand Rapids, MI: Zondervan, 2002).

Turner, Victor, *The Ritual Process: Structure and Anti-Structure* (1966 Lewis Henry Morgan Lectures; New York: Aldine Transaction, 2011).

—*The Forest of Symbols* (New York: Cornell University Press, 1967).

—'Betwixt and Between: The Liminal Period in *Rites de Passage*', in June Helm (ed.), *New Approaches to the Study of Religion: Proceedings of the 1964 Annual Spring Meeting of the American Ethnological Society* (Seattle, WA: University of Washington Press, 1964), pp. 4-20.

Twiss, Richard, *One Church, Many Tribes: Following Jesus the Way God Made You* (Ventura, CA: Regal Books, 2000).

—*Rescuing the Gospel from the Cowboys: A Native American Expression of the Jesus Way* (Downers Grove, IL: InterVarsity Press, 2015).

—'Rescuing Theology from the Cowboys: An Emerging Indigenous Expression of the Jesus Way in North America' (DMin dissertation, Asbury Theological Seminary, Wilmore, KY, 2011).

van Gennep, Arnold, *The Rites of Passage* (London: Routledge, first published 1960, reprint edn, 2013).

Welker, Glenn, 'Chief Tecumseh Shawnee', *Indigenous People*, December 10. Accessed June 2015. http://www.indigenous people.net/tecums eh.htm.

White, James Emery and L. Ford, *Rethinking the Church: A Challenge to Creative Redesign in an Age of Transition* (Grand Rapids, MI: Baker Books, 2003).

Whiteman, Darrell L., *Anthropology and Mission: The Incarnational Connection* (Chicago, IL: CCGM Publishing, 2003).

Wildman, Terry M., *When the Great Spirit Walked Among Us* (Maricopa, AZ: Great Thunder Publishing, 2014).

Willard, Dallas, 'Spiritual Formation as a Natural Part of Salvation', in Jeffrey P. Greenman and George Kalantzis (eds.), *Life in the Spirit: Spiritual Formation in Theological Perspective* (Downers Grove, IL: Inter-Varsity Press, 2010), pp. 45-62.

Zahniser, A.H. Mathias, *Symbol and Ceremony: Making Disciples Across Cultures: Innovations in Mission* (Federal Way, WA: MARC Publications, 1997).

Index of Biblical References

Index of Authors

About the Author

Dr Casey Church is the Director of Wiconi International, a contextual Indigenous ministry based in Vancouver, Washington. He has a Bachelor of Science degree in Anthropology, a Master of Arts in Intercultural Studies, and a Doctor of Intercultural Studies. He is a Pokagon Band Potawatomi member from southwest Michigan. His Potawatomi name is Ankwawango, which means 'Hole in the Clouds'. He is of the Bear clan from his mother's side (the late Mary Church-Pokagon, a Pokagon Band Potawatomi member), and the Crane clan from his father's side (the late Leonard Church, Nottawasippi Huron Band). Casey, his wife Lora, and their five children have lived in Albuquerque, New Mexico, for the past fifteen years.

Casey's journey led him to study traditional spiritual teachings under his Anishinaabe elders. He investigated culturally-appropriate (contextual) approaches to Native evangelism at Fuller Theological Seminary. Casey and Lora pastored a Native church plant in Grand Rapids, Michigan, from 1996 to 2000. Their church was one of the first Native American contextualized congregations in the country. The Churches also ministered with Native Christian ministries in the Southwest.

Casey is a frequent presenter at national and regional conferences on Native ministry and is often asked to be a consultant, teaching his approach to contextual adaptation of Native rituals and ceremonies. He works with the Brethren in Christ Overcomers Alcohol Treatment Program in Farmington, New Mexico, conducting Christian Sweat Lodge Ceremonies and providing guidance in contextual ministry methods. He has served as a consultant and interim staff member for the General Board of Global Ministries of the United Methodist Church's Office of Native American and Indigenous Ministries.

Casey is a board member for NAIITS: An Indigenous Learning Community (previously the North American Institute for Indigenous Theological Studies), a contributing writer for its academic journal, workshop presenter at its symposiums and adjunct instructor at Portland Seminary in Newberg, Oregon.

Wiconi
Removing Barriers, Building Bridges

Learn more about Wiconi:

Wiconi
P.O. Box5246
Vancouver, WA 98668

Email: office@wiconi.com
Phone: 360-607-2599

Website: www.wiconi.com